It's Not About Money…
except when it is

By Amy Dingmann

Dedicated to

the rest of us.

Table of Contents

It's Not About Money…

except when it is

- Intro -

This Isn't a Book About Money

I didn't want to write a book about money.

So, this book really isn't about money—except for when it is.

Although you may find a few specific frugal living tips sprinkled within the text of this book, this book isn't intended to be a massive collection of *15 ways to save money on groceries* or *25 ways to find cheaper entertainment*. You can find that information in countless books already—not to mention on numerous websites—so I didn't want *this* book to be a rehashing of *that*.

At its heart, this book is about all the non-money things that affect how we use money—the way we spend it, the way we save it, and what we actually get from our use of it.

Oh, come on, Amy. Don't get all woo-woo on me. I just want to know how to save some money.

This book is about the simple (but difficult) issues that stand in the way of our living frugally. The things that should be obvious to us, but we keep forgetting—or ignoring them.

This book is also about truth and honesty. It's about the reality that regardless of what financial plan you follow, Life can drop kick you from here to Sunday and ruin your savings.

This book is about the judgment that we all face—and the judging that we all do—when it comes to ours and other's financial lives.

This book is about the conversations we don't know how to have without arguing, and the frustration we feel when money is part of the discussion.

The "solutions" in this book contain many things that people already know deep in their gut, they just need to be reminded in a way they can really hear, in a way that can really soak in and take hold. My hope is to say all of these things in a way that you can wrap your head around them differently than you might have before.

To be honest, sometimes you're not necessarily looking for a financial solution—which works out great because many times there isn't a quick financial solution to share. Sometimes it's enough to hear that others have been in—or *are in*—your same situation. It's hard to take financial advice from someone if you're pretty sure they've never been where you are, or if they've been removed from it so long that their hindsight is rose-tinted.

I am not a money expert, nor do I want to be. If you're looking for advice from someone with a degree in Financial Guruness, that is not me. What I am, however, is a wife and mom and homeschooling farm gal from small town Minnesota who lives frugally—but more importantly, enjoyably—in the midst of the joys and struggles we all know as Life.

I often have people ask me for advice or suggestions: *I need to save money for this. We want to cut our costs here. Tell me how to be more frugal with our spending in this area.*

They come to me, and I figure this can mean only one of two things: either they think I'm a total tightwad miser, or they see we're living differently in some ways and are curious about how they can do it, too.

I'm actually fine with either option.

I know many tricks and tips, but I won't claim to be a frugal genius. I do think, however, that you will find I'm unapologetically real about the topic of frugal living. Since it seems to be the thing to do now, I'll stick a trigger warning on this book as one containing *questions that might make some readers feel uncomfortable*. I'm going to ask you to take a serious look at your life. Not in a way that makes you crunch numbers (although, you might have to do that, too) but in a way that makes you consider some underlying truths of life, like the ability to:

Look at your situation logically; understand that if someone suggests a change to be made, it's not a judgement call on how you live, it's a factual observation.

Own the choices you make. Own the choices you make. Own the choices you make. (I'm repeating myself here because this one is so important, and so ignored.)

Understand not every tip is going to help you. Not every tip is meant for you. But you should be willing to look at every tip that is suggested to you.

Be honest about where you are in life right now, where you want to be, and make peace with the distance between those two things.

Be patient. A huge financial change is often made up of a lot of little tweaks that take time to show results. It's like waking up one day realizing you weigh 450 pounds and deciding you want to be back to your fighting weight of 175. You can't do that overnight.

Through my own life or the lives of those very close to me, I know the sting of words like bankruptcy and foreclosure and divorce. I also know what it's like to have a perfect plan in place to save for something huge and life changing, and to watch that perfect plan be overhauled and replaced and forgotten in a two-steps-forward, three-steps-back sort of dance. When do you finally reach your goal? M-a-n-y y-e-a-r-s after the plan said it should have been reached.

M-a-n-y. Y-e-a-r-s. I had to repeat that because writing it out in a short sentence doesn't really equate to what many years looks like in actual real life.

My hope is that when you're done reading this book, you will feel at least one of two things:

I hope you will feel challenged, because this book asks hard questions about goals and ways to reach them. This book does not dance around the subject of personal responsibility—it meets it head on. It also does not ignore the fact that Life isn't necessarily fair and it cannot be controlled. Life *happens*, and it's not always immediately rectified by having an emergency fund.

I also hope you will feel inspired. This book is partly about learning to be satisfied where you are as you travel the path of where you hope to be.

Amy. Seriously. Don't go all deep on me.

Believe me. I completely understand there are times we just want to know how buy groceries with the lone and sweaty ten-dollar-bill in our pocket. Been there. Done that. Honestly. But if all we ever do is try to figure out how to get through the financial issues of this moment *right here*, we're missing out on how to deal with (or remedy) the financial issues of tomorrow, next week, or ten years from now.

You swear you're not going to get totally woo-woo and drag me out into left field?

Promise.

Folks, it's not about money. Our money issues are often rooted in things that don't have anything to do with coins and paper and plastic. Yes, we need money to live, but life isn't about money and very often our money struggles start when we forget that very simple thing.

I'm trusting you, Amy.

Let's get to it.

- 1 -

"Frugal Living" Can Mean Different Things

Before we get deep into this chit-chat about frugal living, there are a few things I'd like to point out. I think it's best to lay some ground rules, define some phrases, and remind each other why we're here.

Should I grab my coffee?

Yes. Do that. Ready?

What is Your "Why"?

Okay. I know that *what is your why* sounds more like a heady, philosophical beginning to a motivational speech than the start of a book about frugal living by a homeschooling farm girl from Minnesota.

Amy, you promised…

I assure you, there is a point. Don't skim past this. Determining our reason for frugal living is actually necessary—we'll discuss why in a minute. But first, I want you to think about the reason you're actually *on* this frugal journey.

Maybe you want to move to the country and live a more simple life.

Maybe you're in the country and you're trying to figure out how to build a bigger barn.

Maybe you're just trying to pay the electric bill.

Maybe you want to convert your home to solar power and you somehow need to save the funds for those changes.

Maybe you want to see if you can live with less.

Maybe you're trying to figure out how to live as a one income family so you or your spouse can stay home with your kids.

Maybe you're a single parent, just trying to put food on the table.

Maybe you want to cut costs in all areas of your life so you can afford to eat all organic food.

Maybe you live a frugal life because that's what your parents did and it's all you know.

Maybe you seek to live frugally because it's the complete opposite of how you were raised.

The point is we're all doing this frugal living thing for different reasons. We're on individual journeys—yours probably looks much different than the frugal person next to you.

See, there's a big important point about frugal living that is usually ignored in most discussions. And it's something we need to get out of the way before we can actually have a helpful discussion about frugal living.

Frugal Means Different Things to Different People

If you hadn't noticed in the list of reasons above, frugal living means all sorts of different things depending who you ask. Let's divide these people into three different groups. You'll probably see yourself in at least one of them.

Group A:

Some people have "enough money" and are making a choice to be frugal. They're generally not worried about how they are going to eat or that their electricity is going to be turned off.

Maybe they overspent at Christmas, or ran into an unexpected car repair, and now they need to tighten their belt for a few months to cover it.

Maybe they're working on a long-term project that requires saving money—buying a new home or becoming debt free—and that choice has put them on the path of living frugally.

Maybe they just want to break the cycle of living paycheck to paycheck and are looking for ways to make that happen.

Things for people in group A may occasionally be tight—maybe super tight—but when they get down to it, they have enough to cover their needs and can, at times, put extra money towards extra things.

Group B:

Other people have to be frugal because that's what their paycheck (or lack thereof) dictates is necessary. There is no extra. These folks aren't trying to tighten their belt, so to speak—they're just trying to find a pair of pants to put on.

These are the folks who are really scraping by. Who don't have the extra money to put towards a program to help them learn to budget. There is no extra money to put towards savings or make extra payments on an existing bill. If you're trying to figure out which bills to pay this month so you can still eat (or you're not paying some of your bills so you can eat) you're probably a part of group B.

These could also be individuals who already live very simply and frugally, but are looking to move forward financially. As a reader of mine recently pointed out, sometimes it isn't so much a frugality issue (they know how to pinch pennies) as much as it is an income issue (you can only scrimp so much—sometimes you just need more money to work with).

Group C:

These are the folks who would say they are frugal because they don't pay for Netflix, their furniture is old, and they haven't updated the paint in their home with the hot colors of the year. They shop at thrift stores, take on No-Buy Month Challenges, and will continue to drive the same vehicle until they drive it right into the ground. They aren't wrapped up in consumerism and having the latest greatest thing. They're not following trends. They don't go shopping for something to do.

But.

They also pay more for local honey, grass fed beef, and pasture raised eggs. They plant their gardens with heirloom seeds and they buy their baby chicks from heritage breeders, not the farm store.

This group lives simply. They aren't consumed with being consumers, but they're probably spending more in certain areas of life than either of the other two groups put together.

Why the "Why" of our Frugal Living Matters

Popular financial discussions rarely, if ever, bring this up. The reason people are living a frugal life will determine whether or not the popular frugal advice helps them at all. Different groups are able to make different choices, due to the options available to them.

If we're really going to help people with budgeting and frugality, we need to meet people where they are. Frugal tips don't help people if we don't take into consideration where they are on the journey or why they are even there in the first place

Money saving tips like *cut your cable* don't work for people who already don't have cable because they can't afford it. *Stop eating out* doesn't help someone save money if the last time they went out to eat was when someone treated them to a birthday meal.

Eat cheaper food might be a suggestion that works for some, but others aren't going to sacrifice their beliefs regarding health and morality to do so. Ramen is a really inexpensive meal, but you won't generally find it in the kitchen cupboards of someone whose choice to be frugal revolves around simple living with real food.

Most frugal living tips are only aimed at one specific group—which is fine. A tip is never going to help every person it's offered to, and some of us are at different places on the same path. But simply understanding there are people on completely different roads to frugality can give us patience for wading through frugal living advice that doesn't apply to our specific situation.

I mean, when we get down to it, what we all want is just to have enough money, right?

How Much Money is "Enough Money"?

Let's consider something for a moment. When you say, "I wish we were better off," what does that mean? When you look at your journey of frugality, at what point will you be able to say that you succeeded?

When you're not living paycheck to paycheck? When the car payment is gone? When all the credit cards are paid off and cut up?

People often say, "I don't have enough money." How much money *is* enough money?

Because here is the thing. We wish for that spot where we will have enough and be better off. And somewhere along the line, amazingly enough, we reach that spot. Yay! Right?

But what often happens is that, as time goes on, the spot we thought was better off suddenly isn't enough. And we find ourselves reaching for a new *better off*. A new *enough*.

And while some people may say this is simply setting goals, reaching goals, and setting new goals, for many of us it's really just a failure to be satisfied. We want, and we get. And we want, and we get.

And we want.

You know you've done it. I've done it. We've all done it.

Ten years ago, we were all wishing for something. Put your mind in that place ten years ago. What were you

21

wishing for? A more reliable vehicle? A place in the country? To pay off your student loans? To not have to spend every extra penny on diapers and formula?

Now look at your present-day life. Do you have that something now? And have you, as you've moved on with life, simply replaced your definition of *better off* with a different vision of what life should be?

A friend of mine mentioned in conversation once, "Having a job where my income exceeds my needs? Yeah. That'll be the day."

And while we can get all wrapped up and distracted with the *what is a need* and *how is she spending her money* argument, the point is clarified by another friend who once offered that our real issue isn't that we don't make enough money, it is that most of us will never in our life have a job that provides so much income that we'd run out of things to spend that income on.

In other words, when we realize there is space between what we spend and what we could *afford to spend* with what we make, it doesn't take us long to fill that space up with a list of things we need to buy or pay for— intentionally or not.

It's that thing where you get a raise and it seems like you're going to be further ahead…but there is always somewhere that extra money can go, right? And it seems like the more money we have, the more things we find to spend them on.

That doesn't mean we're tossing our extra money away to frivolous things. Not at all. If I suddenly came into some extra money, I would remove the blinders I'm currently wearing about the fact we need to replace our roof. Our house could benefit from siding. If we don't get siding, we at least need to deal with the peeling exterior paint. I would like to get more energy efficient windows. We could use a front door that latches without needing to be body slammed.

I'm sure you can make your own list of things that could be replaced or fixed or purchased. You see, there is always somewhere for the extra money to go. We can make more money and—if stuck with a skewed perspective—never really feel like we're making any headway.

So, for you, how much money is *enough*? And how much money would be *nice to have*? And what is the space between those two amounts?

What We Need to Understand About Frugal Living Advice

Many readers have told me that the tips they see in most frugal living books either don't help them, or don't apply to their life.

So, let's talk about that.

Sometimes it can feel as though the popular financial gurus of the moment are out of touch with Everyday Joe or Jane. And I would even agree with you that in some ways, maybe a few of them are. I mean, if Financial

Guru's Big Amazing Advice is *cut Netflix* I'm going to stare that person down and ask, "M'kay…what else you got?"

But there are few things worth pointing out about frugal living advice that will hopefully help you to have a bit of patience with those who are doing the advising.

There are people who don't know what you already know.

The reason that Financial Guru Extraordinaire continues to suggest something like *cut Netflix* is because there are people who really need to hear that. If there weren't people eating up that advice, it would stop selling. There are people who need to be told that you can eat leftovers and that generic store brands really aren't all that different than name brands. There are folks who need to be told they can put together their own homeschool curriculum and that watching an instructional video on YouTube will help them learn to change their own oil.

We tend to view the financial world through a lens of who surrounds us, or from the community we grew up in. If you were raised in a home where frugality was the norm, advice that suggests shopping at thrift stores or garage sales doesn't help you because it's already second nature. But if you grew up in a home where leftovers bypassed the refrigerator and were scraped into the garbage, there are probably some ways of living frugally you could learn more about.

It has to do with our normal. What is *your* normal? If normal means your child attends a birthday party where everyone goes home with pricy party favors, you're living in a different normal than the parent whose child thinks it's a really big deal to have name-brand macaroni and cheese at Grandma's house.

It's easiest to write for group A.

People in Group A have more options available to them. Because of this, there are more suggestions that can be made to them. Group A contains a larger variety of people in a plethora of situations. While that sometimes means the advice that is offered won't necessarily apply to everyone, it sure gives the advisors a larger group to speak to.

Group A might actually be a little bigger than we'd like to admit.

Some of us have lumped ourselves into group B when really, with some tweaking of our thought processes, we'll discover we're in group A. We might be at the very outskirts of group A, teetering on group B…but we're in group A.

Group B is stripped down. Group B is nothing extra. Group B is scraping by.

Listen. Since this book is about honestly looking at your life, let's do that. I personally would not consider you a part of group B if you can still regularly spend money on…

alcohol, cigarettes, a bottle of pop at the gas station, a caramel macchiato at the coffee shop, On Star, XM Radio, a specific weight loss system, another pet, another purse, another book, another gun, another pair of shoes, more data, in-game purchases, another video game, or wrinkle cream.

Get the picture?

There is a difference between judgment and fact.

I hope you're still with me, because from personal experience in real life conversations, I know that last paragraph probably ruffled some feathers.

We need to get real about the difference between judgment and financial fact.

If the money saving suggestion is, "You would have more money if you didn't smoke 2 packs of cigarettes a day," that is a financial fact. It doesn't mean I'm making a judgment on your smoking habit. It doesn't mean I don't realize it's very hard to quit. It means that if you smoke 2 packs of cigarettes a day—$17ish a day last time I checked here—you're spending $510 a month on cigarettes.

That's a financial fact.

If the suggestion is, "You would have more money if your daughter wasn't in dance, soccer, piano, *and* gymnastics," that is not a judgment on your parenting or what someone feels is the correct amount of extra-

26

curricular activities for your daughter. It means that if you pay monthly fees for your daughter to be in dance ($), soccer ($$), piano ($$$), and gymnastics ($$$$), you're spending $+$$+$$$+$$$$ in extra-curricular fees every month.

That's a financial fact.

We're not all dealing with the same stuff.

While the core tenets of saving money are similar across the board, we need to be honest about the fact we all live in different situations in different areas of the world. Different areas of the country cost more or less than others to conduct life in than other areas of the country, and will pay you more or less than others for doing the same job.

There are many things that simply cost way too much money, and some of those things are required where we live or for the situation we're dealing with.

Some of us started out on the right foot, some of us started out on the left. Simply put, not all of us have the same options available to us.

Sometimes there aren't any more options.

When frustrated with our money situation, we want there to be an answer. We want there to be a solution. We want someone to tell us what to do to loosen up the tight spot that we're in. But sometimes there aren't any more answers or suggestions to give for the moment you're in.

Financial Advice Guru can't make up options that don't exist. If you are frustrated because you don't feel any of the suggestions are helpful to you (and you've honestly considered every and all other possible suggestions), it might be because there simply aren't any more options to suggest to you at this stage of the game.

Like most couples, my hubby and I have gone through our own times of financial yuck. Going through those times meant we had to implement solutions we weren't exactly excited about. They were not enjoyable by any stretch of the imagination, but they were the options we had.

Did I want someone to suggest different options? Absolutely. Did I read frugal living books trying to figure out where we could trim just one more centimeter from our already anorexic budget? For sure. Did we get completely ridiculous in the things we were doing to save money? All the yes. Does that mean there were a ton of options to get us out of where we were at that time?

No. Sometimes things are just hard. Sometimes there isn't enough money. Sometimes you're in a deep, dark valley and all you can do is keep trudging through, hoping to feel the slightest bit of rise in your step each day. And the solution is nothing other than nose to the grind stone, hard work, and a truck load of patience because it's going to take time.

See, the problem is that we buy frugal living books looking for a quick, magical solution, and friends, there isn't a quick, magical solution. There are things we can tweak. There are changes we can make. But a quick and simple magical fix? No.

Sometimes life is hard. Sometimes there isn't enough money. And sometimes there aren't any other suggestions or advice to help. If you're in a tough spot and feel like you can't get the answers you need, this could be the situation you're dealing with. Sometimes the issue isn't that Financial Guru Extraordinaire doesn't have the right advice for you, it's that there isn't any *more* advice to give.

Not really what I wanted to hear, Amy.

I know.

Also, you're welcome.

- 2 -

Less Judgment, More Community

While traipsing around the internet land of frugal living discussions, a comment to an article caught my eye:

"I just want to help people be smarter with their money. I mean, if I can do it, anyone can do it. But the more people I meet, the more I think no one *wants* to be better with their money. It's seriously like people *aren't even trying.*"

Sigh.

This gal will go far in helping people learn to be frugal. What a gem! I mean, I'd *totally* sign up for her course. Wouldn't you?

Some people live frugally and assume they can help others do the same, but spend a lot of their time lost in judgment of the people they're trying to help. A lot of people get stuck on *Jackhole, this is why you suck with money*, and fail to move towards the *here are some actual ideas to help.*

Advising people about money can be a sticky situation. When you point out the things someone could do to change their financial situation, what's your intention behind it? Do you want to help them, or do you want to show them you're more awesome? Do you want to see them improve their situation, or are you trying to backhandedly pound them into the dirt? When you tell someone, *well, here's what I would do*, do you ever follow that up with a humble *do you need help with that?*

The Super Giant "Yeah, But" Elephant in the Room

Wait. Hold up. I know you've got something right on the tip of your tongue. So, why don't you go ahead and let it fly?

Yeah, but… I've tried explaining to my brother/co-worker/friend that they're making horrible financial choices. They ignore my advice and keep complaining about how they don't have any money. Yet, they keep spending.

Yep, I get it.

Let's talk about this very large elephant in the room. That thing everyone is thinking about, and that we need to get out in the open before we can move on. Because until we discuss this, it's going to be the *yeah, but* that people keep coming back to.

Here goes.

There are people who are really irresponsible with money. There are people who complain about not having enough money, and still freely spend on things they probably shouldn't. There are people who will tell you they don't have two dimes to rub together, but then plaster social media with the extravagant birthday gift they bought their wife or husband or kid.

We all know someone like this. Yes?

Here are some things to realize about the phrase *I don't have enough money.*

  a) People have different definitions for the phrase *not enough money.* For some, it means there is only $500 left in the bank account until next payday. For others, it means $5. For some, it means *I probably shouldn't stop after work with friends tonight.* For others, it might mean *I have to brown bag my lunch this week.* To still others, it's *how am I going to fill my car with gas to get to work?*

All of these people would probably use some variation of *not enough money* or being *short on funds* to describe their situations, but they are clearly in different places.

b) Some people just like to talk about not having enough money—just like some people like to talk about football, the struggle to lose weight, or how much they had to drink last weekend. It's a way to join the conversation and fit in.

Then again, some people just like to have something to complain about, and money is an easy way to fill that spot in the conversation, since very few of us ever feel that we have enough money.

In my personal experience of chatting with folks who *aren't* rollin' in the dough, I generally notice a directly *inverse* correlation between how much a person is really struggling and how much they'll freely talk about it.

As in, most people who really don't have two pennies to rub together rarely divulge that information.

But, I get it. It's annoying to listen to people complain about not having enough when we know people in worse situations. It's frustrating to watch folks cause their own financial ruin and then take none of the blame. It's aggravating to watch people play the system or expect a handout. It can all leave a bad taste in our mouth for anyone who professes to not have *enough money*.

So, what to do?

Here's how you deal with people who complain about money and still spend, spend, spend. Or people who ask for your advice about how to budget and don't listen. Or people who play the system and still complain they don't have any dollars.

Stop listening to them.

Seriously.

Stop engaging with them. Or, if you're forced to engage with them, just smile and nod—you know they won't listen to anything you say anyway.

Don't focus on these people. Don't let these people steal your compassion for those who really can use your help.

Every time I talk about people who need help, there is at least one person listening who pulls out the *yeah, but* and goes off about someone they know who is a jackhole with money. As if the fact they know a jackhole means that everyone else's struggles are discredited.

Consider this. We all know a jackhole. We all know a person who is playing the system. We all know that one person who eats more extravagantly with their SNAP EBT card than those who are eating without. We all know a person who complains about being poor while they're on their way to pay for something they honestly don't need.

Blah. And blah blah. And blah.

Hear me now. I want to know that you *really* hear this— those people are not the majority. Exposing them makes a dramatic news story. Memes about them can cause a spectacle on social media. But that doesn't mean they are the majority.

Listen. There are people out there in the midst of hard times because they've put themselves there via choices they've made.

Yes. I said that. I put it here in writing, and I'm not taking it back.

But there are also people who hit issue after issue after issue and struggle to recover, and not for lack of effort or desire. In the midst of their recovery, it's paycheck to paycheck to paycheck—and life is still happening. The furnace stops working. Their daughter wants to go to the overnight choir camp. The water pump goes out on the car. Their son grows again and needs pants.

Think for a moment about the people in your life—not the memes that are passed around Facebook or the group of jackholes that make a good news story when we want to talk about reforming the welfare system. No, the real live folks that actually exist in your community and are struggling with money. Are they struggling because they don't want to get rid of their expensive data plan? Are they struggling because they drive a fancy car with a ridiculous monthly payment they should have never taken on in the first place? Are they struggling because all of their money goes to beer and cigarettes and tattoos?

I know *some* of these people. We all do. And maybe it depends on your circle of friends or where you call home, but the vast majority of the people I know who struggle with money aren't doing so because of a "frivolous" expense they won't give up.

Are there some financial changes we could all make? Sure—and it's worth giving real consideration to any suggestions made in regards to our particular situations. But, having said that, are there components of life that are sometimes just really expensive? Yes. And sometimes there just isn't enough to go around.

I think we are all called to do what we can, where we are, with what we have. That's the responsible, decent human being thing to do.

But realize that when someone is doing what they can, where they are, with what they have, and they run into a financial roadblock, a flippant response of, "Well, that's why I have an emergency fund..." doesn't help anything.

That's nothing against people who have an emergency fund. I think having an emergency fund in place is a fabulous, responsible idea. But not everyone is there yet. Or they had an emergency fund and it's gone—because, emergencies. There are a lot of people doing what they can, where they are, and they still don't have two pennies to rub together. It's hard to build an emergency fund if you're always playing catch-up with life.

We need to learn to talk to people where they actually are, without judgment. And we need to learn to hear advice without feeling that someone is judging us.

What I think a lot of this boils down to is that most of us were never really taught how to have an actual conversation about money.

How to Have a Conversation About Money

Kendra says she's having trouble with money and wants some advice on how to get things under control.

Edwin says, "Tell me what's going on."

Kendra honestly explains her issues. Edwin makes some non-judgmental observations. Kendra shares her goals, and Edwin suggests some things she could do differently. They part as friends.

This is one extreme of a financial discussion: the perfect conversation.

And this almost never happens.

On the other end of the extreme would be the disaster conversations, which we see a whole lot more frequently.

After Kendra explains she is having issues with money and wants Edwin's help, Edwin non-judgmentally points out that Kendra should consider making the choice to stop smoking. Kendra calls Edwin a judgmental jerkface who doesn't understand that tobacco is an addiction. Edwin calmly suggests that perhaps Kendra could pick up another shift at work and she says, "It's like you don't think I'm doing enough already!" Edwin accidentally glances at the new purse Kendra is carrying and Kendra says, "Oh. So now I can't treat myself to anything?"

Well, now. That went well.

Let's look at another scenario.

Edwin makes some suggestions to Kendra like, "Maybe your food bill wouldn't be so high if you would cook from scratch," but fails to realize that Kendra is already working two jobs, and although she really enjoys cooking from scratch, it's not a reality for her right now. Edwin then suggests that Kendra shop at a higher end thrift store for her work clothes, but Kendra can't because she's required to buy uniforms from a certain store. Edwin walks away from the conversation feeling like Kendra *isn't even trying* and Kendra leaves the conversation feeling like Edwin is a complete snob.

When the two people in the conversation are responsible, realistic adults, the conversation can be productive. Edwin can make suggestions to Kendra and she's not offended. She will take an honest look at his advice. But Edwin will also make suggestions to Kendra that are helpful to her own life, not suggestions that are out of her realm of possibility.

See, a big part of the problem is that as a society, we don't know how to talk about money. We know how to *argue* about money. We know how to *complain* about money. We even know how to *judge* other people's money usage. But a good chunk of us don't know how to sit down and have an actual productive conversation about money.

Every so often on Facebook, a chart makes the rounds that shows people how much their family should be spending on groceries if they're *really* living frugally. (Which, by the way, already puts people in an us-against-them, right/wrong mindset).

The commentary, y'all. The conversations in the comments every time these memes show up in my newsfeed are an incredible snowball of judgment and guilt.

"Those numbers are ridiculous. We feed more people for half the amount listed for our family size."

"Those numbers *are* ridiculous. How is someone supposed to eat only spending that much money? Are half the family members not eating?"

"Maybe if you didn't buy convenience food. Try actually cooking from scratch."

"Do you work outside the home? Do you realize most people don't have time to cook from scratch?"

"None of this makes sense. These numbers have got to reflect people who have toddlers, not teenagers."

"This is why we raise all our own meat and have a huge garden. We spend almost nothing on groceries."

"Yeah, but are you adding in the cost of raising your own meat and having that garden?"

Y'all. We don't know how to talk about money because we have so much other stuff attached to it. Our worth. Our place in life. All the arguments for why we don't have as much as we think we should. All the reasons we think people should stop complaining about where they are. All the everything that comes along with how much we *do* or *don't* spend on what. It's all the stuff that says we're hyper focused on our own situation and can't look outside ourselves to see that others might not have the same opportunities. We get stuck there and we spout off our opinions and we're not helping anyone.

Things People Say That Do Not Help Anything

Some people have all the answers. When someone talks about struggling with money, occasionally I'll hear a solution like this:

"Well, if you wanted more money, you should have gone to school for a better career."

Gosh. That's the ticket. Of course!

Okay. Ima respond with a mic this time so people who are saying ridiculous things like this can hear me loud and clear.

Every time I hear this perfect solution to an individual's current money crisis, I think of several of my friends who went to college, graduated with lovely degrees, and then could not find work in their field of choice. Which is weird because they were good, solid career fields.

So, they went to work where they could find work (because that's what responsible people do, right?) but they weren't making what they thought they were going to make with the degree they went to school for. And they started paying back student loans on a degree (because, that's what responsible people do, right?) without the amount of money they thought they were going to make in a job they were supposed to get with the degree they went to school for.

I mean, really. Do you honestly think all the people currently working retail or construction or waiting tables don't have a college degree?

Please.

Whenever I hear this atrocity spewed forth, I also think of the people who were in a good job for a long time and got too far up on the pay scale and were let go. They thought they had a decent job, they were doing what they were supposed to do, and then life drop kicked them off a cliff into a snowbank. *I know you planned to work until retirement age, sir, but the fact is we can hire two people half your age for half the cost. So, you know.*

This is real life, y'all. It happens.

Does that mean these people get to sit back and lament about how unfair life is? No. Life can be unfair, but it also goes on. You need to eat and keep the electric running.

But the fact that half of society is totally engrossed with trying to prove they are financially superior and smart— all the while being totally out of touch with the other half—means we're going to have a hard time helping anyone or each other at all.

Speaking of...

"Food stamps are the problem. Let's get rid of SNAP. The government gives out way too much assistance and people need to learn to stand on their own."

Okay. Fine. Let's do that. I do agree that the government needs to back off.

But, if we get rid of SNAP (the supplemental nutrition assistance program; formerly known as food stamps), here's what it would look like: a lot of people trying to feed their family with the twenty-dollar bill in their pocket.

We want people to be more responsible with their money. We want people to get off assistance. We want people to pay for their own food and utilities. But I honestly think that many people who suggest these things are totally unable to be real about what that would look like.

Are you going to go to the store and help people figure out how to feed their family with the twenty dollars they have in their pocket? Or are you going to stare at them with all of your assumptions and think, *well, if they'd just get a better job...*

Or, *I bet if they didn't spend all their money on cigarettes...*

Or, *I bet they can afford internet...*

Or, *if they didn't spend all their time watching Netflix and maybe learned to cook from scratch...*

All the assumptions, y'all. Stop with the assumptions. We get mad when people make assumptions about the way we spend our money. Let's not turn around and do the same thing.

(And if you're feeling a giant *yeah, but* coming on, please start over at the beginning of this chapter.)

The problem is we need less judgment and we need more community.

Amy, you said you weren't going to do this hold hands around the campfire and talk about our feelings thing…

Hear me out.

I always enjoyed talking with my great uncle who lived through the Great Depression. He died a few years ago, but I remember a conversation I had with him around 2009, when the so-called Great Recession was in full force. We talked about things he and his family had done to get through the toughest years of the 1930s.

The thing he said that I will never forget was that he was worried for our generation going through the Great Recession because we weren't *the people* of the Great Depression. We didn't know what community was. We didn't know how to help *each other*. As a whole, we always depended on someone else to bring the help for ourselves or others.

That was my great uncle. He didn't mince words. He called it as he saw it.

Here's the thing, though. After talking about how all the people he knew got through those tough years because of all the ways they helped each other, he pointed out that there were people who wouldn't help. He remembered very clearly a family who had no time for helping anyone. They were above everyone else. They had a judgmental way of looking at everyone's struggles. In the true spirit of my great uncle, he had some colorful language to describe this family that hadn't lived far from them.

And then, this particular family hit rough times. Their struggles came full force and they found themselves in the same situation as all the community around them.

And you know what? No one helped them.

The rose-colored lenses of looking into the past usually makes us think of how helpful people were and how they sacrificed to assist their neighbors. And many times, they were and they did. But my great uncle pointed out there were such limited resources between everyone that they certainly weren't going to share them with someone they knew wouldn't reciprocate. There just wasn't that much to go around.

And as I tried to keep hold of a fading fantasy built around ever-helpful folks of the Great Depression, my great uncle said, "The truth is, Amy, you'll waste your time and your resources trying to help people that aren't willing to help themselves."

I sorta felt like I'd listened in on a secret *True Tales of the Great Depression* story time. And I've chewed on that tale for a very long time. There are so many lessons in there that I think we are completely missing today.

My personal opinion—if it matters—is that it's not the government's job to assist people with their finances. I think when the government gets involved in people's lives, it leads to a lot of issues (many of which we're talking about in this book). But in order to not have the government's help, the people have to be willing to help each other.

There are always going to be those who need help. The poor will always be with you. So, the question isn't whether or not the government should help, it's that if the government doesn't, are *we* willing to step in?

Yeah, but…

See, there it is again. The *yeah, but*. So here. Let's go over this again.

There are people you will help and they will appreciate it and will pay it forward or you know they will be the kind of people who will help you out some way if you were to need it.

There are also people who always need help and always take and you start to get the impression that if you were ever in a bind and needed help, they suddenly wouldn't know who you were or would have every excuse under the sun to explain why they aren't the right ones to help you out.

These are two very real types of people that have existed for all time.

I believe it is our job to help people, but I think there is a certain way to go about it. The way I see it is this:

> a) Take the first step. If we're always waiting for someone else to step forward, no one ever does.

> b) Get to know people. Get to know their situation. Offer to help them in a way that you can handle helping them *that will actually help them.* Sometimes giving them $20 isn't the best answer. Sometimes it is.

> c) Assess if your help is really helping. That doesn't mean be judgmental. We are all given a certain number of resources in order to help other people. This book revolves around frugal living, so your first thought might be money. But money is not the only thing we have to offer each other in times of need.

> d) If your help isn't helping them, take your help elsewhere. I believe we are called to help people, but we need to define what help is. If I'm spending my time giving help to someone who has no inclination to change their situation, that means I don't have that time to spend helping someone who actually does. I would hate to think that person A (who has fallen on hard times and just needs a little bump) can't be helped by me because I'm in month 6 of helping Person B who

has proven they have no desire to take any steps—not even a tiny one—to show they are working towards something different. I don't think that's being judgmental, I think that's being honest. I think that's being a good steward of the resources I have.

e) If you determine your help isn't actually helping, move on. As in, don't dwell on it. As in, don't turn the situation into fodder to feed a belief that all people who hit hard times are worthless.

f) Stop looking for a trophy. Help because it's the right thing to do.

Keep your judgment in check. Create community, and help the people around you. But remember, you can only do what you can do.

And if ever you feel yourself building up another *yeah, but,* go back and start this chapter again.

Or, if you're brave enough, swirl this sobering bit around your tongue: since we all have different values and things we deem as important when it comes to money, it's completely possible that in some way, *you* are someone else's *yeah, but* example.

Ouch, Amy. Ouch.

Yeah. You're welcome.

- 3 -

Stop Buying Stuff You Don't Need

If we're going to talk about saving money, the thing we really need to discuss—boring and predictable as it may be—is how to cut back on your spending.

Cutting back. For real, Amy? Tell me something I don't know.

Take a hard look at your life. Take a serious gut punching look at your life. Go ahead. Knock the wind out of yourself. If you're looking to save money, answer this question: where can you cut back? Look at your budget. Look at the things you spend your money on. Where can you trim?

And then, just because I like to keep it real, what do you need to be honest about that you could trim but are not willing to trim?

That, friends, is what we need to talk about.

Defining a Want and a Need

Sometimes we try to make a want into a need. As in, "I need to protect myself, so therefore I *need* this Kimber 9mm." Or, "My chickens need shelter so therefore I *need* to order this $2500 custom built chicken coop."

No. No, you don't.

You don't need those things any more than I *need* a brand-new Ibanez blue sunburst electric acoustic guitar—even though it would be really nice for playing at church services.

If we want to get hardcore, we really have very few needs as it relates to purchases. We need food to eat, water to drink, somewhere to protect us from the elements, and clothes to do the same. We know this deep down in our gut. This is elementary school stuff, right?

When You Spend Money, Own the Choice You've Made

There were two fears I had when setting out to write a frugal living book, the biggest of which was this: someone would walk into the local grocery store and start assessing the contents of my cart. Or stalk me on social media to judge the things I was spending my money on.

Oh sure, she writes about how we need to save money, and there she is taking a selfie at Dairy Queen again. Sure. Yeah. Whatever, Amy.

Contrary to what some might think, my purpose here isn't that you stop spending money all together.

Seriously. It's not.

Let me repeat that: my purpose here is not to turn you into some miserly penny pincher who feels completely deprived and hates life because Amy said you can't spend any money. That's not my purpose at all. The purpose is to help us be honest about the way we view and use money so that we can realistically reach whatever goals we have.

If you're going to buy stuff that you don't need, be honest about the fact you don't need it. Which is to say don't buy a coffee at Starbucks every day and then complain that you don't have money to pay your bills.

If you want to keep 7 cats, 5 dogs, and a tank of saltwater fish, that's your choice. But it costs money. And when someone suggests—for the sake of cost efficiency—that you cut down on the pets, the fact that you shake your head no is a choice. Own it, baby. Own it.

It's your choice to go to the jewelry parties or the leggings parties or the cooking supply parties, especially if you know that you can't possibly attend without being convinced you need to buy something. Own it.

It's your choice to meet friends at the bar after work or the coffee shop on the weekend. Yes, even if it's to blow off steam or it's how you get some time away from the kids. Own the choice.

I'm not saying any of these things are bad. I'm not saying you shouldn't do any of these things. This is not to say you shouldn't treat yourself. This is not to say that you shouldn't pay for a haircut or buy the more expensive honey from a local beekeeper.

I *am* saying that all of these things are choices with a financial result.

What I'm getting at is this: everyone makes choices regarding how they use their money, and money issues can't be solved until you're honest about the way you spend and the reasons behind it.

Let's Be Clear: Not Everyone Wants to Save Money

While some people look at their life in frustration because they want to cut all of the corners in order to save all of the money, others take a different approach. One reader was very blunt with me about his reasons for spending.

"I know we can save money if we change the way that we spend. But you know what? I'm okay with spending. I grew up in a family where we didn't have a lot of money.

I now have a decent job with decent pay and I am going to spend that money on my family. We are going to have things that I didn't have and we are going to do things that I didn't get to do."

And that's fine.

Again, I'm not saying spending is bad. I'm not saying that buying things is wrong. Spending money is fine as long as you have the money to spend. Spending money is totally acceptable as long as you own up to what you're spending and why.

The issue comes in when people want to cut costs or save money and aren't owning up to what they're spending money on. When out of one side of their mouth, they complain that they don't have any money and from the other side, they're purchasing a pair of heels in a different shade of black or a subscription to a coffee-of-the-month club. You know these folks. On Monday, they're totally committed to a budget, but by the time Friday rolls around, they've bought a brand-new boat and are looking at a bigger truck to haul it.

I will point out, however, that once again, the above-mentioned reader is dealing with an issue that seems to be about money, but isn't really about money. It's about making up for experiences he didn't have in his childhood. It's about providing something for his family that he didn't feel was provided to him.

So, you see, spending or saving, it's still not about the money.

Want to Save? You Need to Stop.

If you want to become more frugal, here are a few things you might want to stop doing.

Stop Shopping for Something to Do

If you are trying to save money, cut costs, be more frugal, or simplify your life, you need to stop using shopping as a form of entertainment.

I'm even talking about garage sales or thrift shopping. Do not fool yourself into thinking that just because you shop at a store where things are discounted that you're somehow doing something noble and are excluded from this warning. Before you walk into the local thrift store, stop and ask yourself: what am I actually looking for? Wait. Am I looking for anything? If not—and you are trying to save money—do *not* go into the thrift store.

Seriously. Pull your car out of the parking lot and move on.

Because here's what happens. You find something you didn't realize you needed or wanted and it comes home with you. It might be:

- a book that looks really interesting (that you don't have time to read).
- a shirt that would go with that one pair of pants (that you're never going to wear anyway because seriously—where would you wear them?)

- a perfectly priced grab bag of yarn (that you can't use until you locate your long-lost knitting needles).

The thrift store is full of so many things and you need them all, right?

No. No, you don't.

I didn't know I needed you until I found you might be a romantic verse in a love song, but it's not helping anyone's bank account.

I mean, can you imagine Ma Ingalls climbing up in the wagon and riding to town just to look in the shops for something to do?

"Charles, the girls and I are going to town to go shopping…"

Hear me now, friends. If you're on a mission to save all the dollars and you are still shopping as a form of entertainment, please stop. If you're heading into the store and don't have a clear purpose for being there, turn around. Go home and sit on your hands until the urge passes to pull out your debit card for a little swipey-swipe action.

But, Amy! My friend has a cute little occasional shop where she sells jellies and hand painted signs and homemade soap and crocheted bits of magicalness! I want to support her, so I shop there. There's nothing wrong with that, right?

Let's not overthink this. Yes, support your friend. But support her because she has something you need to purchase. Buy the hand painted sign because it's the perfect gift for your mom, not because you are going to bring it home, set it in the corner, put some bags in front of it, and forget you even bought it.

Stop Spending Money to Fill Yourself Up

Some people experience this at Target. In fact, it's so common there are memes and videos about people walking into the store intending to buy toothpaste and toilet paper and coming out with $457 worth of other stuff—ultimately forgetting the toothpaste and toilet paper.

And while it's sorta funny, the longer you think about it, it's actually really not funny at all.

Some people might view this as *I walked into Target and was just overcome with the awesome of all the things I needed and they were all right there in front of me!*

What amazing timing you have. I mean, how lucky are you?

Sarcasm aside, this buying of all the things is a way deeper issue. Some people go on a shopping spree and it's kind of like a sugar high. They feel really good when they purchase things. It makes them feel powerful, taken care of, important, decorated, and awesome. But, like a sugar high, it doesn't last very long. It's a cheap high that costs a lot of money.

If you're spending money to fill an emotional need or a void in your life, stop. If you're spending money because you're bored, stop. If you're spending money because it makes you feel superior in some way, stop.

Just stop. Okay?

Stop Spending Money to Fit In

We joke about the desire to fit in as being school-aged stuff. It's something we're supposed to outgrow, except that some of us don't. We just spend more of our own money to do it when we're older.

"A bunch of gals in my homeschool mom group were doing the gluten free thing," Tina said. "So, I decided my family would do it, too. At first, I didn't think about the extra cost because we had plenty of money so it didn't make a difference. It's weird because it was almost like all these moms were eating this same diet as a way to bond with each other. Like, it was what made us the group we were."

But Tina, her husband, and their five kids suddenly hit one hard patch after another until they found themselves in a situation where they didn't know where their next paychecks would be coming from.

"The thing I realized almost immediately," she said, "was how much stuff we'd become accustomed to buying as a *need* that was easy to take off the list when the money wasn't coming in anymore. I just kept thinking why were we spending our money on this? Why does it seem so necessary to buy that stuff to fit into that group when it's so easy to give it up when the money isn't there?"

For Tina, it was "the gluten free thing," which she confessed had nothing to do with health and more to do with wanting to be part of a group. As in, her friends were doing it so she wanted to do it, too.

There are many things that zip through society as the latest fad. Some diet or creative endeavor or way of living becomes the latest greatest thing and people want to partake in that thing—and it almost always has a financial cost.

Be honest about your reasons for participating. We can do that now, you know. We're adults.

How to Fight Temptation

So, how do we stop buying the stuff we don't need? It's all about fighting temptation, baby.

If you're tempted to spend money while you're out and about (or, let's be real—when you're buzzing around online) here is something I like to suggest.

What is your goal?

It's much easier to resist temptation when you have a goal. It's easier to fight an urge if you have a solid thing you're working towards. So, what is *your* goal? Are you saving for a house? Are you trying to get rid of debt? Do you want to take a family vacation? Do you simply want to have some money in the bank?

The goal has to be something you really want—
something that actually holds importance for you.
Otherwise, at some point, the temptation will outweigh
your desire to reach the goal. It's the same reason we
fail at dieting. If you're not hardcore committed to losing
35 pounds, that chocolate caramel cheesecake suddenly
becomes overwhelmingly tempting.

If it helps, try to visualize your goal

Amy. Stop.

I'm serious. If you're saving money because your end
goal is a farm, find a picture of a big red barn or Sophie
the Chicken and slap that bad boy on everything you
can—your phone case, your desktop background, in the
refrigerator, on the dash of your car…everywhere. Look
at this picture every time you feel the need to buy
something. Look in to Sophie's chicken eyes and ask her
what she thinks about your potential purchase.

Sophie won't steer you wrong.

A reward can help.

Some folks need a little extra oomph on the way to their
goal, especially if they know it's going to take a good
chunk of time to reach that goal. Saving money to buy a
farm is a much longer journey than saving money to
replace your vacuum.

(Side note: how many of you scoffed at the thought of
saving money to buy a vacuum cleaner? The last

vacuum cleaner I bought was $175. I mean, you weren't going to put that on a credit card...were you?)

If it encourages your purposes, it's completely okay to build in some rewards along your frugal living journey. Obviously, it doesn't make sense to reward yourself with something that sets you backwards. I wouldn't reward myself for saving $1000 by spending $500. But I would maybe take myself out for ice cream after sending off the final payment on a loan or reaching a certain balance in my savings account.

Continue to live.

There is no joy in saving money or living frugally if you're denying yourself everything.

But, Amy. The title of this chapter is stop buying stuff you don't need. Now you're just a hypocrite.

No, I don't think so. We all have to find that fine line between saving money joyfully, and living a frugal life that makes us want to stab out our eyeballs with a fork. While living frugally, you still need to *live*. It's still important to be joyful on the way to your goal.

Part of the problem is that some of us feel like we're supposed to live in a land of extremes. As in, we either have to be miserly and not spend a dime or we should spend freely and toss the Benjis around like rock stars.

Here's a spoiler alert: most of us live in the middle ground. Most of us will *always* live in the middle ground. And that's okay.

When you do *nothing* extra, you will sputter out on the way to reaching your goal. Saving money and living in a financially responsible way doesn't make a whole lot of sense to me if there is no joy in doing it. So yes, be responsible. But if the ice cream truck pulls up while you're out on a family walk in the neighborhood, it's okay to drop a few bucks every so often.

Remember, spending money isn't wrong—if you have it and it makes sense in relation to your goals.

- 4 -

Save Money on Stuff You Do Need

I tried to ignore the issue, but as usual, ignoring the issue didn't make it go away. In fact, the issue just got bigger until one of the kids asked, "Is it just me, or is the bathroom ceiling changing color?"

When we moved to the farm, we added a shower to the bathroom where there had previously only been a tub. However, it became apparent that the original bathroom fan couldn't keep up with the humidity from a shower and thus began our problem with mold. Or, as the boys called it, *the ceiling that sorta looked like pink camo.*

Grumble. Is it just me or does this stuff always seem to rear its ugly head just when you were getting ahead in pinching pennies?

The bathroom ceiling needed to be cleaned and some sheetrock needed to be replaced. A larger fan had to be installed, and then everything had to be re-painted. Do I know anything about replacing a bathroom fan? Nope. Totally clueless. But we figured it out and did the work ourselves.

Trust me. Nothing says *romantic date* like sheetrock dust and some ductwork that looks like a giant slinky.

But hey—that's one way to save the dollars.

As we move through life, there are items we need to own. There are things we need to pay for in order to live where we do. And as luck would have it, there are usually things we need to fix or replace—the cheapest last-ditch option often being more than we'd like to spend.

Welcome to adulting.

Dealing with Things We Are Locked Into

When I surveyed readers about their biggest expenses, the most common answers were their mortgage, health insurance, and gasoline.

One reader commented, "It's kind of weird, though, because most money saving tips don't have anything to do with saving money on mortgages, health insurance, or gasoline."

Dear reader, you are completely right. I've noticed that, too. But there is a very simple reason for this.

There aren't a ton of ways to cut costs on your mortgage. Once you're in the house, there isn't much you can do to save on your monthly payment other than refinance or move to a cheaper home.

As far as saving money on health insurance—that's one ginormous razor toothed slippery shark that I'm not going to touch with a 20-foot pole.

When considering the cost of gasoline, you can drive a more fuel-efficient vehicle (if you can afford it) and consciously combine errands when possible. But for the most part, people need to drive where they need to drive to, and gas costs what it costs.

The bigger purchases that most of us have to deal with are often things we are more or less locked into. Some of those things we got locked into when we were in a different financial situation, or had different financial goals we were working towards.

But there's an easy fix, right?

"Your mortgage is too much? Sell your house!"

Come, now. That works great, if the housing market is moving. But sometimes that advice is easier to roll off the tongue than to see it actually come to fruition.

A good friend of mine was recently shocked to find out that her particular insurance policy was going to increase by several hundred dollars per month when she added her teen sons to her auto insurance. Yes, she got quotes from several companies. Yes, she shopped around for the best deal. Yes, her sons had good grades.

Some things just cost a lot of money in the specific circumstances you're in.

So, the reason we save money on all the other smaller things? Sometimes it's so we can have the money for the bigger things that we're more or less locked into.

Know What You Spend

You might hear me repeat this one a lot. Please don't feel like I'm being condescending or beating you up, because I repeat this one to myself as well. Tracking what you spend takes work that is sometimes boring and monotonous and I fall out of practice, too. But you aren't going to know if you're saving money on something (or that you *should* be saving money) if you aren't keeping track of what you spend.

Be honest. 9 times out of 10, your best guess about what you spend is nowhere near what you actually spend.

A gal stopped me in the grocery store once. There was a sale on a certain kind of cheese and she asked me—as I was loading up my hands—if it was a good deal.

"I mean, I usually buy the store brand cheese," she said, "but I don't really pay attention to what it costs."

Look at the costs, you guys. See what you're spending. Know what's coming out of your bank account.

I'm totally serious. Track your spending. Track your spending. Track your spending.

Okay, Amy. I get it.

Good! And now that you're going to track your spending, we can talk about those things you need to buy.

Questions About Things You Need to Buy

When faced with those things that you need (or strongly desire) to buy, there are some questions you can ask yourself to help decide about the purchase.

You need/want it, but do you need this specific one?

It's sitting right there in front of you, and you *could* buy it, but is this the best one to buy?

Shop around. Check out clearance sections, thrift stores, and online markets. Research brands and read reviews.

Pro tip: before you buy anything on Amazon or other online retailers, read the reviews. That's why they are there. I can't tell you the number of times I've talked to people who were unhappy with an online purchase who would have not chosen the specific product they'd bought if they'd just scrolled a bit further to the customer reviews.

And let's be clear, even though we want to save money, sometimes the cheaper one isn't the best choice.

Sometimes the cheaper one is going to break in a week and you'll be back to the drawing board.

But let's also be clear—sometimes that cheap one is the one you can afford.

You need/want it, but do you need it right now?

My oldest was looking for a bass guitar, and he saw one that he fell in love with. And while I wouldn't consider this a need by any stretch of the imagination, he certainly did.

His brother tried to convince him to look around, but he purchased in the heat of the moment and brought that baby home. Could he have saved some money by waiting? Maybe. Could he have found something he liked even better? Perhaps.

We all know what happens to the Valentine's Day chocolate or Christmas decorations the week after the holiday passes. Isn't it amazing how the value of something can change according to the date on the calendar, even though the actual thing hasn't changed at all?

There are items that go on sale certain times of the year. For instance, many people say that you'll find better deals on bedding and linens in January, while June is the best month to purchase home gym equipment. Pay attention to the calendar. It's similar at the grocery store. Fruit and veggies are less expensive when they are in season, and seafood is always on sale during Lent.

You need/want it, but do you need your own?

I recently read an article that pointed out how back in the day, only certain people had threshing machines. The farmer who owned the machine would travel around to neighboring farms so everyone could use their machine.

Would it have been easier and more convenient to have your own threshing machine to use whenever you wanted? Well, sure.

But did everyone actually *need* their own threshing machine? No.

What if only a couple people on your street owned zero-turn lawnmowers? Or wood splitters? Or chainsaws? Or pressure canners?

It's a relatively new concept that we all have these bigger, more expensive items sitting in our garage or shed or house.

But I get it. Life is different now. If everyone works 9-5 jobs away from home, that only leaves Saturday and Sunday (or the occasional night, if you're not running your kids to practice) for most people to mow lawn. If there is only one lawnmower on the block, how in the world would all the mowing get done in the hours you have available?

That's a big part of the reason why people started owning their own things. Convenience.

Convenience costs money. Consider if you could share ownership of something with another party.

You need/want it, but do you need as much?

Coffee and me, we're totally BFF.

But we need to talk about my BFF and how much we're seeing of each other. And since I know a lot of people have a BFF named Coffee, (or Coke, or Ice Cream, or Wine) I decided we could chat about this.

Coffee. I drink a lot of it. And although I love it, it might actually be one of the reasons I'm not quite reaching some of my goals. Here's the thing. This whole coffee thing? You're wasting money. Seriously. You're wasting money. Did I mention you're wasting money?

I'm wasting money, Amy?

Let's sit down together and figure out how much you're spending on your little friend, Coffee, every month.

Go ahead, I'll wait.

Okay. So, one of two things probably happened.

- You dropped your coffee mug because you really didn't realize how much you spent between running to the coffee shop, or accidentally stopping at the coffee shop, or making 37 pots of coffee a day and having to buy more beans, or...
- You're saying, "Seriously, Amy? I only spend like $16 on my coffee every month, which is

small beans compared to the folks who get a venti mocha at Starbucks every day."

Regardless of how you answered, I'm going to challenge you—because *anything* that you use less of will last you longer. And anything that lasts you longer costs you less because you're replacing it less.

You stop at Starbucks every day? How about stopping once a week? Or twice a month? You go through a bag of coffee beans in half a week? If you drank less, that bag of coffee beans could last you a whole week. Or two weeks. Or a month. And the money that you're saving could be put towards...what? A new kitchen sink? Replacing those broken tiles in the bathroom? More sturdy tomato cages for next year's garden?

And I get it. I love coffee. I mean, I really love a good cup of joe. *Hear me now, sweet Jesus, I love coffee.* Always have, and always will. But part of adulting is knowing when it's time to say, "You know what? Two cups of coffee a day are plenty for me."

We all have goals, and a lot of those goals require some amount of money in order to be reached. What are your goals? And how much faster could you reach them if you took control of your coffee addiction? If you enjoyed a morning cup of coffee instead of a morning pot of coffee followed by a second breakfast of the same?

I know it doesn't seem like a big deal because coffee seems small in the scheme of things, but big things are made up of little things. Big changes start with baby steps. We're all at different places on the path to our goals, and we've all got vices that stand in our way. Every little thing you do to loosen the grip of that vice brings you closer to having the resources you need for the goals you're trying to reach.

Why Sometimes Your Efforts to Save Money Don't Help

You may think that cutting down on coffee consumption is being wicked hardcore. Or way over the top. And maybe it is.

But if you frame things correctly, it can help you get where you need to go.

Frame things correctly?

Listen. I know people who are rinsing out their plastic bags to re-use and saving drawers of twist ties because dude, they are *frugal*. Which is fine. But the crazy thing is that they have no problem dropping $8.54 on two donuts, a soda, and a bag of chips every day on the way to work.

There are a couple ways to look at this. Either they are a) being super frugal in certain areas because it frees up money to spend elsewhere, or b) they just don't realize that things don't add up.

I would be willing to bet money that most the time, it's option b. Being really frugal in some areas and totally careless in others and *not realizing it* means you're not getting ahead.

This, you guys. *This* is why we don't get anywhere. We're standing in the grocery store agonizing over the cost difference between two different laundry soaps— because we could save $1.29 by going with the cheaper, less effective soap—but we're thirsty at the checkout so we grab a 20-ounce pop for $1.49 to keep us satisfied on the three-minute drive home.

This why we're stuck. We're trying so hard to save money in some areas, and we don't realize we're spending it in others. It's like we're robbing from Peter to pay Paul, but we don't even comprehend that we're doing it.

Are you going to talk about tracking our spending again?

I don't have to. You just mentioned it. You're catching on.

Actual Tips for Saving the Dollars

Years ago, I tripped upon *The Complete Tightwad Gazette* and thought I'd won the lottery. The book, a collection of monthly newsletters originally published in the 90s by Amy Dayzcn, was chock full of hints and tips for living a frugal life. It used to sit on the end table in our living room and was pretty much my frugal living bible.

But times have changed. Now we have the internet, which most of us carry around in our pocket. You don't have to wait for a paper newsletter to arrive in your mailbox in order to find the tips. In this new age of constant information, you go looking for the tips.

Alas, this wouldn't be a money saving book without giving you *some* money saving suggestions, although a quick trip down the rabbit trails of the internet will give you a plethora of tips to choose from. There truly is nothing new under the sun, but I've included some of the things we regularly do in order to keep our costs down, as well as a few tips from my readers who were kind enough to submit them via social media. Here goes...

Think About It and Talk to Each Other

When you need or want something, write it down in a central place so everyone can see it. If I'm clueless that my husband is planning to fix the air compressor and needs a $45 part, we really can't budget well. Likewise, if he doesn't know that the printer needs ink and the dog is due for a rabies shot, he's going to think we have a different amount of spending cash than we actually do.

"We have all of our bills in a spreadsheet. Every two weeks, pay day, we have a money meeting. We pay them together and talk about any extras we need/want at that time. We both know exactly where we stand for our bills, savings, and extras. I used to handle all the money myself and there always seemed to be extras that added up too much, like eating out. Now we both know what we have and what our short term and long term financial goals are. Simply working together and dedicating specific times to sit down together has made a big difference for us. We are finally able to save money instead of wasting it on things we didn't even realize before." — Colleen F.

"For us, the best *tip* isn't really a tip, it's a mindset. Needs versus wants, short and long term. It really helps to identify where you are looking to be and whether a purchase of any kind brings you closer to or further away from your goals. It's big picture thinking versus instant gratification...." — Julaine V.

"The most important way to save is changing your thinking. Stuff is just stuff. I have reduced much of my spending by owning only what I really need or really love. The way I cut my spending was this - I don't place the value of an item on whatever the price tag says. The value of the item is *how many hours did I have to work to earn that money?* Three hours of work sounds a lot more expensive than any dollar amount." — Kim C.

"My wife and I budget pretty much every penny so we can make it with her working just 15 hours a week instead of the 40 she was so she can be with our young kids more. But we also know if we don't have some kind of frill through the month, we will go crazy. Her frills are different than mine. [For example] Starbucks versus a movie theater. We each get 50 dollars in blow money to spend on whatever we like, no questions asked. The rest is budgeted and if we are going to buy anything other than gas or groceries we tell the other beforehand so we can check on *do we actually need that.* Also, combined accounts and no hidden money or accounts. Everything is together and open for accountability." — Alan P.

"When I'd like to buy something I don't need urgently, I give myself a week to think about it. Often in that week, I figure out a way to use something I already own for the same purpose, or I even decide I don't need it that badly." — Meghann R.

Use Technology to Your Advantage

The internet is truly amazing. Do you ever just stop and think about how insane it is that if you have a question, you can speak it into your phone and get the answer back, along with hundreds or thousands of articles and videos?

I realize this amazement probably only occurs to half of you, because if you're even slightly younger than me, you were born into an age where this amazement is just normal—like how to breathe or drink water. Humor us. Sit quietly while I explain the powers and total okayness and acceptableness of using the interwebz for everything.

Twelve or so years ago, I remember being in an old-fashioned living online forum, and someone lamenting that they felt such a dichotomy between simple living and using the internet. The way she saw it, internet was technology and simple living was *not.*

All these years later, I'm not sure that people even think about that anymore.

I mean, when you don't know how to do something, what's the first thing most of us do? We punch up our ol' friend Google or YouTube and let them tell us how to do it.

Confession: YouTube is where I learned to can and preserve food. It's how my husband figures out how to fix things that he doesn't have experience fixing. It's how I learned to cut my kids' hair. It's how I learned to cut *my* hair. It's how I learned about building a fodder system. It's where I go when I need to know a cheap fix for something in the basement or how to build something for the barn.

The internet is full of people sharing their knowledge and experience and hints and tips and a good chunk of it is all out there for nothing more than whatever you pay for internet access. Since you're already paying for it, the internet should be your first stop—not an afterthought—when you have a question or need an explanation.

Knowledge is power. We are in an unprecedented age of information. Use the internet to your money-saving advantage.

Dress Yourself

It goes without saying that shopping the thrift stores, garage sales, and clearance racks are great ways to save money on clothing. I'm in my late 30s and I still have no shame in accepting hand me downs from friends and relatives. Except for undergarments and socks, I can't remember the last time I bought a brand-new piece of clothing.

Beyond that, my save-the-dollars-on-clothing tips are simple:

Only buy clothes that fit you and that you like. It is better to have 14 outfits in your closet that you feel awesome about than 45 outfits that only strike your fancy when the stars and moon align correctly over your house. Not only will this save you money, it will save you from trying on 15 different outfits when it's time to go somewhere.

Wives: your husband will totally thank you. Husbands: you're welcome.

Buy clothes that can be worn with other clothing interchangeably. Do not buy a brand-new pair of bedazzled hot pink stilettos because they go with *that one outfit.* I will add the caveat here that I am not a clothes horse. I am not fashionable. I'd be totally happy in the same pair of jeans and a sweatshirt for a week, but that also goes along with the life I live. The chickens don't care if they see me in the same clothes every day. I realize your boss at the insurance office might think differently.

Having said that, you still probably don't need the hot pink stilettos.

Stay the same size. If you are constantly losing and/or gaining weight, you will be constantly buying clothes. Figure out what size works best for you and commit to it. I'm not saying you need to be a size two. I'm saying if you're really made to be a size 10, but in the process of dieting/not dieting you swing from a six to a 14, you're not doing yourself, your closet, or your bank account any favors.

Kids and Money

This might seem counterintuitive, but hear me out. Even though it will cost you money, I *do* think that kids should get an allowance, and here's why.

The only way that people learn how money *really* works is by consistently working with money. It's not by sitting in a class. It's not by filling out a worksheet. It's not by taking a field trip to the bank. It's not by getting birthday money and blowing it on a toy.

But your kids will learn how money works with a weekly allowance. Now, whether you tie an allowance to chores or not is your deal. We do, but that's just how our house works. But with an allowance, your kids will learn to save. They will learn how long it takes to work for something they want. They will also learn what happens when they blow all their money.

Here is the thing, though. For them to really get how this works, you have to stop buying your kids things at the store. The coffee, the pop, the candy, earbuds when they blow theirs—all the little extras.

I wouldn't say that my kids were ever whiny and needy and un-frugal, but I do think there is truth to the fact that if you're not the one buying something, you really don't understand how much it costs.

So, while this does add an extra "bill" to mom and dad's bank account, I think it's a great way to teach your kids how money works. I consider it a worthy expense.

Get in My Belly

Stop counting calories and start counting pennies. Which is to say you don't always need a second helping. If you only have one helping now, you can have the leftovers for lunch tomorrow. That, my friends, saves money. Bonus: it works whether you're growing your own food or shopping at the grocery store.

Stop taking expiration dates as God's truth written in stone. Long ago, people used their five senses to figure out if food was still okay to eat. I am of the firm belief that people still have that ability. If you honestly think that your Italian salad dressing is bad because it's one day past what the stamped expiration date says, you've fallen victim to the marketing game that is *this food is old and needs to be replaced.*

"Buy foods and stock up when they go on sale at buy one, get one free. Half price food! Can't beat that!" — Rebekah S.

"My husband and I don't mind cooking so on date nights we 'Grocery Store Splurge' instead of going out to eat. We buy whatever we want to eat and drink that would usually be out of the grocery budget, and we never spend as much as we would going *out* to eat." — Melody L.

"Stock your pantry with food specifically for those days you would normally run to a restaurant, so even when nothing is thawed out or planned, there is an emergency dinner ready on the shelf, and *way* cheaper than eating out. For my family, it is spaghetti *in* rather than eating *out*. I don't have spaghetti on our typical menu planning, so it is a welcome change when I need it to cover a failed dinner plan." — Sonja A.

"Making our own bread. I know it sounds really bizarre, but it helps to keep us committed to making homemade food instead of eating out, which helps keep us in budget." — B. Forrey

"Don't buy tomato juice. Here a can of juice is $1.29 or more. A can of tomato paste is $.25. I add 5-6 cups water and a teaspoon of salt...tomato juice!" — Grace B.

"I have many tips that I have learned or made up myself over the last 48 years of marriage. I have a new love though, it is Boston Burger. Boston Burger is 60% ground beef and 40% ground pork. I buy it at Food 4 Less for less than $2.00 lb. It makes the best burgers, meatballs, meatloaf, etc. you will ever eat. We also love beans of all kinds here, so I cook them in bulk in the crockpot and freeze them in quart bags. I never have to buy beans in cans for any reason now and refried beans made with them is way better than canned from the store. I love to thaw and heat them up with different seasonings and use as a side. I make my own BBQ pork, beef, and chicken in my crock pot. I shred it and freeze it in quart bags to use whenever I need something really quick." — Jane P.

"I've always had a 'regular' coffee pot, not one of those single serve expensive things. I never buy coffee. I make a pot and take a to-go cup with me—or a thermos if it's going to be a while. I don't understand why people pay anywhere between $1-$5 for a coffee." — Nancy M.

Oh. Speaking of coffee…

When it became easier to make coffee, people started to drink more of it. So maybe what you need to do is go old school and percolate that coffee on the stove. Another option is to use a French press, which means you have to boil water in a tea kettle and then steep the coffee grounds in the press. Both choices are more involved than just pressing a power button, and that may be the key to cutting down your consumption—which can also help your wallet.

And if you *are* going to use a single cup coffee maker, for the love of all that's logical, choose the reusable basket for grounds or the refillable coffee pods so you're not dealing with the ridiculous expense of those k-cups.

Yes. I said it. *Ridiculous* expense.

If you're really crazy, you can just drink hot water. I know this sounds nutty—like totally insane—but I have found that when I'm reaching for a cup of coffee, what I'm actually craving—especially in the winter—is a hot mug to hold on to with some hot liquid to swallow. Many times, I've found that hot water does the trick. Which works out pretty well because our water happens to be free.

Getting' Pretty and Cleanin' Up

Cut your own hair. Seriously. Or find someone who knows how to cut hair that you can barter with. Or treat yourself to a once a year haircut to get things all spiffy and then do your darndest to keep it up at home. Choose a hairstyle that doesn't require as much upkeep. This might mean you need to be a little less trendy, but yo. You're still totally hawt.

Or, you can do what this farmgirl usually does—put on a hat or a bandana.

"Shop at dollar stores for cleaning supplies and other necessary items. Instead of spending $50 (or more) a month, I usually spend $15 or so. Helps keep me on budget." — Chrystal B.

I'm also a fan of baking soda and vinegar. You can buy them in bulk and you really *can* clean a whole lot of stuff with them. Add blue Dawn dish soap to your bag of tricks and you're pretty much unstoppable.

Take It Outdoors

Whether you're in the yard, the garage, the barn, or the garden, there is always something that needs to be dealt with. How does one save money on *these* things?

"I fix everything to the point of being ridiculous. I figure, if I succeed in patching those pants or reviving that lawn mower, then I save myself the money. If I fail, then I just got myself a lesson on how to better repair it next time." — Jessie G

"I use my cardboard style egg cartons to plant seeds." —
Ann B.

"Use the 'junk' you find when moving to an old farm
house. I know that we found so much stuff when moving
in to a run-down farm house that needed a lot of work.
But, we have taken advantage of so many of those piles
of junk! Metal piles were welded into fence panels for the
pigs, an old auger system was taken apart and the
buckets were used to create feeders, old cabinets were
stripped down and repainted to make furniture that we
now love—the opportunities are endless! I know, trust
me, I *know* how much you want that junk gone so you
can start living and building *your* home, but be creative
with the things you find and it will save you a lot of
money in the long run! You don't need all brand-new
stuff, especially when you are first starting out." —
Caitlyn H.

Life costs money, y'all. Learning how to save money on
the things you need (or want to add to your life) is one
way to stay ahead of the game.

Or at least *in* it.

- 5 -

Use the Stuff You Buy

In the simplest of comparisons, our houses are twice the size of houses a hundred years ago—which is crazy, because most of us have families that are half the size of a hundred years ago. Why the need for all that extra space?

Two reasons, spelled s-t-u-f-f and c-l-u-t-t-e-r.

We've already talked about not buying stuff that we don't need, right? *This* chapter is about dealing with the storehouses of stuff we *already have*. All the goodies we shoved into our homes before Amy cleared her throat to remind us we don't need to be buying *all the things*.

All the Stuff We Have

We all have plenty of stuff. But the issue isn't really how much stuff we have—this is not about minimalism or reducing our possessions to a certain magical number. The issue at hand is whether or not we can use the stuff we have. If we can't use it (or don't want to use it), why do we have it?

There are two ways to head off the issue of having too much stuff:

> a) stop spending money on stuff you're realistically not going to use—you know, the thing we talked about a couple chapters ago—or

> b) start actually using the stuff you spend your money on.

That *using the stuff you spend your money on* is why you will find me standing ready—however unenthusiastically—in stretched out yoga pants and a mismatched sports bra, waiting for the day's workout to appear on the television screen.

It's not that I like to workout. I mean, I like what working out does for me. I know in my head that when I spend a lot of time writing (read: sitting) it's important that I get up and move. I even understand that working on the farm doesn't necessarily work all my muscle groups and it's still a good idea to, you know, workout.

But I don't really like working out. I almost always have to convince myself it's a good idea. So, what is it that keeps me working out to the DVD?

It's because, at one point long ago, I paid money for it. And this particular workout system DVD wasn't cheap.

What Stuff Do I Even Have?

It's very sweet and homey and simple to say "use what you have". And we all get what that means. In fact, you might assume I'm going to take you down the path of *your chipped plates are just fine* and *the crackly speakers are good enough* because you should just *use what you have.*

Nope. I'm gonna take a different path. I'm gonna go a little deeper here in the argument and point out this reality: most of us *don't even know what we have* to use.

There is a phenomenon that many a mother will witness after telling her kids to clean their rooms. When the kids actually do it, they discover all this stuff they didn't know they had, and they get right to playing with these newfound treasures. The magical thing is that these newfound treasures are things the kids have always had the whole time—the treasures have just blended into the stuff in their rooms.

Now, let's not be too judgmental of the kiddos. Because if we're honest, y'all? That describes many of our houses—whether we have kids or not.

All the Stuff You Don't Realize You Have

I would love to believe that I use most of the stuff that I own. And maybe you would, too.

But here's the thing.

Walk around your house. Choose one room. Look at one area of that room. Really focus on the items that are there. You've probably spent money on most of them—or they've been gifted to you or you bartered for them. Regardless of how you got an item, *something* was usually exchanged in order for it to become yours.

Really take a look—I'm serious here. Because what happens is that the things that surround us sort of blend into the background and just become part of the scenery. Much like a kid who no longer notices the stuffed animal propped up in the corner of his room, we no longer see the dusty binoculars, the box of half-finished model cars, the space heater, or the clipboard with all the fodder system plans—which, by the way, are all things I'm currently looking at in my own living room.

It's the magazine you subscribe to that is sitting under a stack of other magazines that you keep meaning to read but never quite get to.

It's the app you paid for to help with your productivity that you're not using.

It's the book you loaded on your Kindle that you meant to read (that you're going to read!) that you haven't read yet.

It's the case of canning jars you bought that is still sitting in the basement because between all the other things you have going on, you haven't gotten around to using them.

It's the basement shelf full of Blu-Ray discs that you aren't watching. They're such good movies that you won't get rid of them, but every time someone wants to choose a movie to watch, you stream another new one from Amazon.

It's the candle you bought because it looked nice and smelled pretty and you haven't even burned it yet because you're in this weird hoarding thing where you feel guilty that you even bought it and somehow burning it will make that worse. So, it's shoved in the cabinet under the bathroom sink collecting dust.

Truth be told, we all have a lot of stuff in our houses that we're not using. My guess is that on this little escapade you found many little treasures you had flat out stopped noticing in your home.

Stop playing with them now, though. We've got some more talking to do.

There are generally three reasons to explain why you haven't been using that treasure you just found.

> 1) you never actually needed the thing in the first place,
>
> 2) you needed it at one time, but don't anymore, or,

3) you didn't realize you had the item because of disorganization and clutter in your house.

All the Clutter

There is a popular decluttering method that requires holding on to each item you own and deciding if it brings you joy. Now, that might be a little woo-woo for some of us. I mean, I can't see my husband going out and touching each and every bolt, piece of bailing twine, roll of duct tape, oil changing pan, or garage poster, and considering whether or not it brings him joy.

But there is something to be said for checking out every item in your possession.

I like to take a similar but less flowery approach which is this: pick up an item. Determine if you've used it in the last 6 months (12 months if it is a seasonal item). If you haven't used it, get rid of it.

Seriously. I mean it. And I'm going to tell you why I can now say that without reservation.

While searching for our farm, we rented my parents' basement. It was supposed to be a short-term thing that ended up being a four year gig. During that time, most of our own house was in storage. Here's what I'm going to tell you about that. If you're storing stuff for 4 years and you open that storage locker and do not remember most of the stuff you had stored in there, it's probably a good clue that you can get rid of a good chunk of what's being stored.

Now to be honest, there were a few things we re-discovered and kept because when sharing a home with another family, you don't really think much about the dishes or bath towels or furniture you aren't using (because they aren't needed) while sharing another space. But I will also be honest and say there was a lot of stuff we found and did not remember at all. When it came time to move to the farm, my husband and I went through boxes in storage repeating the mantra *if we haven't used it in four years and it isn't something we need at the farm, get rid of it.*

Y'all, I never considered us to be a family that kept a lot of random things, and even *I* was surprised after going through the storage area. We actually owned a lot of stuff that we didn't use. We put together boxes *full* of things that we parted with.

I can't imagine the process for other folks who are keepers of all the things.

Two Common Reasons People Want to Keep All the Things

You are sentimental and can't get rid of anything.

It's hard for some people to part with stuff because they're super sentimental, and they are overtaken by guilt. They feel like they should keep it—even though they know they're literally never going to use it. They know that when they die, it will be that thing their kids clean out of the house, saying a) *I didn't know mom/dad ever had one of these*, and/or b) *what in the world are we supposed to do with this now?*

Ready for some honesty? I've met a lot of adult children in this exact situation who ultimately solve the above issue by making a very large drop-off at their local thrift store. Is that why you're buying and saving the items? Because they will look great on the shelf at the local thrift store several decades down the road?

You're a prepper and feel that piles of stuff help you be prepared.

I can hear the cries of the prepared. *I need to store stuff so I can have it on hand! I need to keep stuff because that's how I'm ready for everything!*

Yes. There is that. I get it, because I store certain items, too. But I hope we can all adult and decide whether or not the pile is for later possible usefulness or it's a useless pile of stuff that will threaten to take over your property.

But…how can we determine which it is, Amy?

I'm so glad you asked. Because here is the honest to God truth: you can't use something if you can't find it.

You Can't Use Something If You Can't Find It

Let's say you choose to save an XYZ because you know someday you might need it.

Years later, you're in a situation where you need XYZ. You don't realize you had XYZ because your pile/shed/garage/basement/closet containing XYZ is so cluttered and disorganized, you couldn't have found XYZ if you tried.

That, my friends, means you have a useless pile of stuff.

That's not to say the *things in the pile* are useless. It simply means your pile of stuff *isn't usable as is.*

Y'all, we need to get organized.

In the town I grew up in, there was a small local hardware store that was piled top to bottom with stuff. Walking in was overwhelming—there was no way the average Joe or Jane would find what they were looking for. But if you asked the owner or his family where to find a bike tire inner tube or a bag for grandma's old upright vacuum cleaner, they could tell you how far down in what aisle, how far up on the shelf to look, and what it was sitting next to.

It was truly impressive.

But let's be honest—most of us are not that knowledgeable about what is in our house, garage, barn, or on our property.

If you don't know what you have, you can't use it. If you aren't aware that you already have something and you purchase another one, you've wasted money. You've literally bought double.

This doesn't just refer to items that are somewhere in your house that you're saving to use someday. This also refers to that pair of BDU pants you one-clicked online, and discovered upon receiving didn't quite fit right. That pair of pants you intended to box up and send back. The pair of pants that was buried under another box of lawnmower parts and science curriculum that got stashed in the office when company arrived. The pair of pants you found a month later and discovered the exchange time had elapsed. Now you're stuck with a pair of BDU pants that don't fit, *and* you have to order another pair.

What about rebates you forget to send in because they're buried in your purse? Coupons you clipped but misplaced before leaving for the grocery store? Frequent customer reward cards that you can't find so you can't enjoy their perks?

Trust me: there is an undeniable connection between disorganization and wasted money.

You Can't Use Something If It Doesn't Work

Look. They don't make things like they used to. Things break. But if something breaks, for the love of all that's holy, try to fix it before you toss it aside. If there is any value left in the item and it's cheaper to fix it than replace it, fix it. Again, sometimes things are so cheaply made that it's actually less expensive to buy another one than fiddle with fixing the old one, but a lot of people *assume* this is the case before they even contemplate fixing the item themselves.

Part of being able to use what you've spent money on is having the skills to fix that thing if and when it breaks. You know, "use it up, wear it out, *make it do*, or do without."

But what if I don't know how to fix it, Amy?

You can't fix it? Says who? Before you tell me you can't fix something, I want you check a little website I've heard of called YouTube. In this great technological era we live in, you can YouTube or Google anything and discover that almost always, someone has made a video about how to fix that broken thing you're holding.

You can also use social media to ask all your people if anyone knows how to repair the item you're dealing with. Technology, when used correctly, can be a great way to help you save money.

Getting Rid of the Stuff You Don't Use

After you rediscover the many things in your house you forgot you owned—and after you're done playing with them—you have two options:

> a) You're going to keep the item because you know you're actually going to use it, or,

> b) You're going to get rid of it.

Do not feel guilty when you get rid of things you're not going to use. You have an opportunity to pass that item along to someone who *does* need it and *will* use it—which is the only place that item should be passed along to. Someone who needs it. Someone who really actually honest to goodness needs it or would like to have it.

Do not pass your unused items or things you don't want on to someone else to clutter up *their* homes. We don't want to perpetuate a cycle of filling up other people's homes with stuff they don't need that someday they will need to declutter and pass on to someone else who doesn't really need it…so on, and so forth.

You Have to Follow Through

Sometimes using what you have isn't completely about stuff or clutter. It's more about making a decision to do something and then following through because money was spent. It's a class you sign up and pay for but elect not to go to for whatever reason. It's a premium website or app you pay for that you're not taking full advantage of. It's the sewing machine you had to have, but are a little intimidated by, so you haven't quite got around to using it.

And we're all guilty of it, author included. Here—I'll prove it again.

I recently toyed around with the idea of adding a podcast to my websites. When I mentioned this to my husband, he thought it was a great idea. However, since my current office was in a room that was a noisy pass-through from the main entrance to our home, he suggested what I should really do is move my office to the other side of the house where there was less traffic.

Tucked into the southeast corner of our home is a lovely room that was mostly unused (seeing as how our boys had since moved beyond needing a room to hold all their little kid homeschool supplies). It was quiet and actually had a door that closed! This, yes *this*, was the room I would turn into my office.

We all worked together to make this office-on-a-budget completely awesome. The boys built me a new desktop computer to replace my old laptop—the one that sounded like it could vibrate right off my desk at any minute. We built a large corner desk instead of buying one. My husband and sons went forth and ordered me all the (budget friendly) equipment I would need to make a decent podcast, as well as a tripod for shooting videos. Things got fancied up.

Honestly, it freaked me out a bit since even though we were going the budget route, we were still spending r-e-a-l money.

And then everything was done. And I sat in that office. And I looked at that podcasting equipment and thought, *now what*?

It would have been very easy to come up with a billion and two reasons for not starting my podcast—the first of which was that I sorta had no flipping clue what I was doing. I loved listening to podcasts. I liked the idea of making a podcast. But did I have any clue how to actually go about making one? Kinda. But not *entirely*.

I had a choice to make right there. I could come up with more excuses about why that boom arm and mic and pop filter would just collect dust, or I could sit down at that desk and figure out *exactly* what I was doing, and then *do it*.

And you know why I went with option two? It wasn't just because I was overcome with warm squishy love feelings for a husband and two sons who merely heard me mention I was interested in something, and did whatever they could to make it a reality for me.

It was also because, yo, that new office and all that equipment cost real, actual dollars. We bought the stuff, so it best get used.

Friends, figure out what stuff you have and then *use the stuff you have*.

Do it.

- 6 -

Be on the Same Page with Your Spouse about Money

Money is one of the most common things that a couple will argue about over the course of their life together. And while it's easy to dismissively suggest that these things should have been discussed before marriage, the truth is many of these issues don't surface until years later.

Men and Women (Sometimes) Think Differently About Money

When it comes down to it, money means different things to different people. In a relationship, money and the concept of having it can represent various things. These contrasts can make discussions about money difficult not because of how much income a couple has or doesn't have, but because of the deeper things represented by that income.

Generally speaking, men tend to think of money as a way to provide, while women often view money as security. And yes, this goes for workin' women as well. When asked about their views regarding the money they bring home, their answers more often revolved around it having made them *feel secure* rather than giving them a sense they had *provided for someone*

That's just what my research turned up. Please don't send me hate mail if it's not true for you.

Does it work to put those two views of money together in a relationship?

Maybe. Sorta. Depends on how you look at it. As one reader of mine pointed out, "My husband wants to spend money because it makes him feel like he has provided for me, but I want to save that money in case of an emergency. This often is the reason we get into arguments, and it's frustrating because really, we can both see both sides."

The other problem is that when money is tight, it's not just that things aren't being paid for or that you have to go with less. It's that *generally speaking*, a man will feel as though he's not providing, and a woman will feel like she has no security. Those are deeper emotional issues to deal with than the simple fact of how much is or isn't in your bank account.

Remember, it's not about money…except when it is.

One acquaintance tells that when she and her husband were first married, they didn't have a lot of money. Living frugally was their normal and they didn't think anything of it. But seven years into their marriage, he completely changed careers and suddenly brought home a significantly larger income. While one might assume this would have had a positive effect on their marriage, it was actually when their issues began.

"Things we never would have thought to buy or be involved in were suddenly part of our life. He wanted us to go out and do all these things because we had the money. He thought he was giving me a better life. But I was more than happy to stay at home doing things that were cheap like we had before. He was always crabby and hurt that I didn't like his gifts. I was crabby and hurt because it felt like he'd changed. I remember asking him once, *why is the money so important now?* And he told me, *because we never had it before.*"

"When my wife and I were dating," explains another reader, "I always tried to buy nice things for her. I mean, you do that when you're trying to woo a gal, right? It continued on for a bit after we got married, but then life took over. There were bigger bills and a mortgage and a kid right away. There was less money. She told me one day that she felt forgotten because I never bought her flowers anymore. I told her I could pick her some from the front yard. I seem to remember that she didn't speak to me for three days after that."

Let's face it—we can talk about frugality and budgets all day, but some of us just aren't on the same page as our spouse. What if money is the thing you just can't agree on? Here are a few conversations that were shared with me by my readers. Maybe they sound similar to something you've dealt with.

"My spouse and I are completely at odds about everything having to do with money. What to save, what to spend, what's important to even have in the first place."

"I'm tired of my husband acting like I'm taking all the money. All I'm doing is paying the bills. It's like he thinks there is more money somewhere. If he knows of some hiding spot, I sure wish he'd tell me..."

"What I don't get is how if she wants something for her quilting, we drop everything to buy it. But if I want something for a fishing trip, suddenly there isn't any extra money. That gets old, really fast."

"He wants me to be in charge of paying the bills but I think that's only so he can be mad about the fact there's hardly any money left after I pay them."

"We both have full time jobs. Somehow it seems her money is her fun money and my money pays the bills. And I guess that set-up could work...if my money is going to pay all of *our* bills, her money should go to pay for all of *our* fun."

So, what is the right way for you to deal with finances as a couple? Answer: The way that works. And this is another one of those things where we want there to be a quick answer. As in, *this is the issue, here is your solution.*

But it's not always that easy.

I'll say it again, it's not about money—except when it is—and many times the reasons that couples disagree about how money should be handled is because of something deeper than the actual money issue.

"My wife doesn't want me to be in charge of paying the bills in our house because her father paid the bills in their house growing up—except he was actually taking all their money and gambling it away. My wife has huge trust issues when it comes to money and wants to be in charge of running the finances. Now, I don't have any control issues with that...but I will tell you something, she's not good at finances. She doesn't want me to be in charge of the money because of 'stuff' leftover from her father, but we're going to lose our house if she doesn't figure out how to pay the bills on time. And when I tell her that, it makes her feel like I'm trying to control the situation—just like her father did."

Finances can be tricky to handle as a couple, especially if there are underlying issues. The truth is, there isn't one way that works for every partnership. While many couples are successful with a joint bank account, there are also many couples whose households run more smoothly when they have separate accounts. For instance, I know married couples with separate bank accounts who have divided the household bills between the two of them. They are each responsible for certain bills within the household and when those bills are paid, the rest of the money is theirs to do with as they choose—separately. Some couples even have three accounts: a his, a hers, and an ours, with different purposes for each account.

The point is that different things work for different couples, especially if they are dealing with specific issues or personalities. If a certain set-up works for them financially (and emotionally), who is anyone else to say their financial set-up is wrong?

Speaking of Bills and Bank Accounts...

So, let's take a look at your house. Who pays the bills?

Clarification: I'm not asking who makes the money. I'm asking who actually sits down and makes sure that the money gets to all the bills it needs to pay on time. Who is in charge of the household budgeting? Who balances the bank account?

Now, let's be very honest here. Assuming you didn't answer *both of us*, does the other half of your partnership know what the bills are? Does the one who isn't in charge of the bills know how much is going out every month? What's coming in every month? What you're spending on groceries, heat, car insurance, Netflix, and violin lessons?

No?

I figured. Don't worry. It's totally common.

Actually, just kidding. You *should* worry.

Ignorance might be bliss but it can also lead to misunderstandings and disagreements and money wasting ridiculousness resulting in someone sleeping on the couch.

It's important for you both to know what's going on with the household finances. If one of you is in charge of the budget and you know how every single penny is spent, you've got a totally different perspective on the budget than your Other Half, who might just have a general idea of what's going on in the bank account.

While both of you might be aware of how much money is coming in, if you're not discussing your household budget and finances, half of your team is in the dark. Only the person in charge of the bills knows how much money is going out, and whether or not that number works together nicely with what's coming in.

A friend remembers a time early in her own marriage: her husband would bring home his paycheck, she'd put it in the bank with her own paycheck, and then she would get started on paying the bills. It was a set up that seemed to work just fine, since her husband really wanted nothing to do with the headache of sitting down to pay bills. And everything *was* fine…until it became apparent her husband thought the money should be going further than it was.

"What do you mean we're already out of money?" he would often say, and remind her how much his paycheck had been.

If you don't know what the bills are or what your household costs to run, you might be shocked to find out how much of your paycheck is actually required to take care of it.

I'll say it again: you both need to know what's going on with your household finances.

Regardless of whether your household is run from a joint bank account or separate accounts, it's still very important that you both have a feel for what the total financial picture is for your shared household.

Tips for Adulting About Money with Your Spouse

Let's put this bluntly. If you can share a bed with someone, you can most certainly share conversations about money and how to use it. Here are a few suggestions about how to start dealing with the money issues in your household. Spoiler alert—they all have to do with communication.

Amy, seriously?

Seriously.

Write down everything you need.

This is absolutely my #1 tip. If there are things you need (or want), write them down in a central place. This can be as simple as a dry erase board in the dining room, or as technological as an app that gets shared with your spouse.

Here's why: I couldn't tell you when the next time is that my husband will be changing oil in his truck or getting a new blade for the chainsaw. Likewise, he really doesn't keep tabs on when I order seeds for our garden or homeschool curriculum for our kids. I don't know what piece of farm machinery he will be modifying next. He has nothing to do with what feed I bring home for our farm animals.

The point is this: while neither of you have to necessarily care what the other person is doing with all that vehicle or garden stuff, you should both be *aware*—because all that stuff costs money.

I once heard two male relatives joking about not telling their wives about how much they'd spent on some garage project because their wives just "didn't need to know about that" and it "wasn't any of her business, anyway." And this is nothing against guys, because I've heard wives joke about clothes they've bought and hidden in their closet because their husbands "just don't need to know about that" and it "isn't any of their business". It's like we all have this need to joke about how much *control* our partner does or doesn't have over us.

I mean, ha-ha. Super funny.

Truly.

But honestly? It's lame. You're in a partnership, not a secret competition. If one of you spends all the money on tools or purses or ammunition or leggings, neither of you (not to mention your kids) will be eating.

Talking about purchases has nothing to do with not being able to buy something without asking. This is not about being controlled or hen-pecked by your partner. It has everything to do with being accountable to each other for the purchases you're making because you share a home and a life and a goal. Or, as I like to call it, being part of a mature healthy relationship.

Honor the fact that one of you wants to spend some extra funds on a new table saw. Honor the fact that the other half of you wants to spend some extra funds on a new sewing machine. You're both adults. Talk amongst yourselves and figure it out.

And if you can't? Well, once again…that's a "money issue" that really has nothing to do with money.

Shop together at least once.

One of you probably does the majority of the household shopping. Not that both of you should be able to rattle off how much you spend on laundry soap in a month, but it sure helps to head off some arguments if one of you thinks the next necessities-only trip to Walmart will be $30 and the other knows it will be closer to $150. For some people, the difference between the two amounts is an annoyance. For others, it's an overdraft.

Hit the grocery store on your next hot date and take a gander at what things cost. It could be an eye-opening experience.

Talk. A. Lot.

It's good to discuss money stuff. Remember what I said about sharing a bed?

Get it all out in the open. What are your plans? Where do you want to be this time next year? What do you think your biggest issues are with saving and spending?

How hardcore do you want to go…and are you both on board with that? What about that vacation you take in the summer? What about that gun you were going to buy? What things will you still be spending on and what things will you quit tossing your money at? What will you do when "something comes up"?

Do you need to build in some rewards along the way, or will you just plow ahead? What is your timeframe for accomplishing this goal?

Dim the lights, put on some nice tunes, and…you know, talk about money.

Help keep each other accountable.

Recently my husband and I sat down to figure out what bills we would pay off with our tax refund. By paying off those bills, it freed up a certain amount of money each month. We knew that if we took that amount of money and applied it to the other bills that weren't yet paid off, we could pay them off quicker.

My husband looked right at me and said, "Yeah, but will we be disciplined enough to do this?"

I loved his honesty. Here we knew what we should do, but at 40 years old and 17 years of marriage, he was honest enough to look at me and question the reality of it. It was going to take work, and sometimes we wouldn't want to do it. Sometimes we would fail. And we'd have to pick ourselves back up and keep going if we wanted to reach our goals.

Honesty is important, and that's why I share this conversation with you. My husband and I live frugally, but we sometimes still struggle with not spending all the dollars. We're human, and I think it's important you know that. I'm not a financial guru sitting on a hill in a multi-million-dollar home. I'm a farmgirl who lives frugally 95% of the time. The other 5% of the time, I really want to hit a Starbucks.

Every single Kindle book or prime movie that is one-clicked adds up. Every gas station pop or coffee shop latte adds up. Holding each other accountable means it's okay to say, "Are you sure you really want to buy that?"

Figure out how you best like to shop.

Are you more frugal with cash or a debit card?

Some people spend less if they use cash. They might have a mental thing about breaking large bills. It's also easier to see what you've spent when the actual paper bills are leaving your wallet, and that can be a bit convicting.

On the other hand, others spend less with a debit card. A friend tells that she still thinks of debit cards as plastic and she grew up with the notion that plastic was never pulled out unless it was for an unusually large purchase or an emergency. With some of that stuck in the back of her head, she generally finds she won't swipe a card for less than a certain amount.

What if talking doesn't work your issues out?

Some of you might be thinking *that's great, Amy. I'm glad you can sit down and have a conversation about money with your husband and figure things out. I tried to talk to mine, and he basically laughed and told me to take a flying leap.*

Look. I can sugarcoat this but I don't want to waste anyone's time. Dealing with money in a shared household, whether or not you have joint accounts or separate accounts, requires some amount of teamwork. There is no magic wand that can be waved to fix these issues. It takes conversation and hard work. And if one or both members of the team aren't willing to have the conversation or commit to the work, friends…that's *not* a money issue. It's something else entirely.

Just sayin'.

Start talking to each other about money. Get on the same page with your spouse about goals and how to reach them. It's certainly not the sexiest conversation you'll ever have, but without the conversation, it may kill what's happening in the bedroom.

Because, let's face it: one of you sleeping on the couch makes it a pretty boring evening for the both of you.

- 7 -

Make Peace with Yourself and Where You Are

I used to have the loveliest hair—an almost white, glimmering shade of blonde that came from days on end spent outdoors and, you know...youth.

My hair color now? I hate it. It looks like dishwater that needs to be changed. The last time I treated myself to a haircut, the stylist said, "I mean, your hair is blonde, but it's like... *dirty blonde*."

Yeah. Thanks.

I have three ways I can deal with this.

> • I can dye my hair, which I have done. But when you dye your hair, you have to keep dyeing your

hair. And if you're going to keep dyeing your hair, you have to be honest about the fact that it isn't a need—it's totally a want—and it's taking money away from other things.

• I can stop looking in the mirror. This would work. I think we only have two mirrors in our house and I could easily bypass one of them because it's on a corner wall behind a bedroom door. But not looking in the mirror doesn't get to the heart of the issue, really.

• The best way to deal would be to just make peace with it. I'm not 20 anymore. There are a lot of things about me that aren't what they used to be. I could simply get over myself, accept the fact that I've earned this dirty blonde hair by my years of (ahem) *life experience*, and move on.

It's time to make peace with where we are in life. Stop worrying about what others think about your hair, your clothing, your cart of groceries, or your frugality. Seriously. We all—author included—need to stop caring what they think. I mean, who are *they*?

As a farmgirl, I would estimate my closet as follows: 80% clothes for around the farm, 20% clothes for church. I can't tell you how many times I've stood in front of my bathroom mirror getting ready for church and, after lamenting about my dirty blonde hair, start playing through possible scenarios and conversations brought on by my choice of clothing. You know, that 20% of my closet that I just keep cycling through until the outfits get a snag or a stain or a hole I can't fix and are moved to the farm pile. And I just keep praying people won't notice that I probably wore this same shirt and pants only four Sundays ago.

But here's the thing. Do you remember what Mrs. Andrews wore in church last week? Mrs. Nelson? Mrs. Potter?

No, you probably don't. And you know what?

None of them remember what you wore either.

Listen. When we're prepping to go out to church or work or lunch with friends, we stare in the mirror and hyper focus on ourselves. Kind of hard not to do when you're staring in a mirror. But here's the thing: we don't realize it, but we assume other people are hyper focused on us as well.

As in, if *I'm* hyper focused on the fact that I just wore this shirt last Wednesday when I picked my kids up from confirmation and my shoes are really scuffed and I maybe should have at least put on some lip gloss, I'm assuming that *you* see, and know, and care about all that stuff, too. It's my fear. Like I'm letting it all hang out and everyone else is pointing and laughing and going home to talk about my fashion choice while they enjoy tea and finger sandwiches.

But they aren't doing that. Seriously. 99% of the world is worried about their own shirt and shoes and don't have the brain space to care about mine. (And if for some totally messed up reason they *are* going home to talk about your clothes, that's a comment on *their* lack of awesome, not yours—and you can't do jack about their issues.)

Getting Mental About Ditching the Joneses

There are psychological ramifications of having to live frugally—especially if it's not how you were raised, or it's a change from how you've lived previously as an adult. Those psychological things can sometimes be hard to deal with.

When you can't go to the party or the fishing weekend or be involved in Secret Santa or the volunteer project or the missions trip because you're trying to save money— or because you straight up don't have the money in the first place—it can be frustrating.

Here is something that people don't understand about being successful at frugal living. It's not just about saving money. Frugal living is not just about spending less. Part of frugal living is being content with not having everything. Not in a way that is part of a fad or looks good as a blog post. Frugal living only lasts if you can find a way to be content with having less when living with less becomes your normal.

We waste money keeping up with the Joneses. And let's be clear, keeping up with the Joneses doesn't always mean you have to drive a certain car or live in a house that boasts a certain square footage. The Joneses can represent something completely different in various social circles.

We can get gooshy and discuss why we are trying to keep up with the Joneses. We can ponder what we think is missing from our life and what part of our soul we are trying to fill or what fear we are trying to calm with the things we are purchasing.

Let's not, Amy.

Okay. But I want to bring this to the level of the people who are usually ignored in financial advice circles. Because when most articles talk about keeping up with the Joneses, they are talking about exotic vacations and art collections. For many of us, that's not real life. For many of us, that's not anything we're ever going to (or necessarily want to) attain. So, we shut off and shut down and stop listening.

But you know what? We're still trying to keep up with the Joneses.

Or maybe it's the Marks or the Schlegerts or the Antiguas. It's why we pay the $35 entry fee so our kid can run in the local 5k with his friends. It's why we bring cupcakes from the good bakery to the birthday party. It's why we buy a raffle ticket to a fundraiser that all the other parents are participating in.

We're all trying to keep up with the Joneses for the same reasons that everyone always has, regardless of the dollar amount on their annual income. It's status. It's fitting in. It's to impress others with what we can do. It's to influence what people think about us. It's to be part of the in-crowd.

Look. Some cool kids buy yachts. Other cool kids buy canoes. The dollar amount doesn't matter—the reason behind the purchase is the same.

The Blessing of Tough Times

"I actually think that people with extra money make more bad decisions than those without. People with more money just have a buffer to recover," says my good friend and cousin, Diana. "When I worked at a bank and made a steady income instead of commission sales, I would run up to the grocery store and get whatever I needed whenever I needed it. Trash bags for $2.99 were no big deal."

"Now," she continues, "my income is different and I'm looking for a better deal. I went to the Dollar Tree and found better trash bags for a buck. What if I had gone to the Dollar Tree the whole time I worked at the bank and put those two dollars in a savings account or something? Sometimes it takes being down to know how to live when you're up."

Good advice. Unfortunately, most of us don't remember the lessons we learn when we're down.

A friend and I sat across from each other enjoying coffee and conversation. Our chit chat skittered across job loss, health insurance, food prices, how to fix mold growth in a bathroom, and kids who wanted to learn piano.

"You know," she said, "I hate to say it, but I almost think we do better when we have less money. When times are tough."

I knew what she meant. When times are tough and there isn't any money (or you stop spending credit, or you don't have any credit left to spend...) you tend to realize just how creative you can be. I've often thought that the washings I can get from a single bottle of shampoo is directly correlated to how little money I have in the bank account at any given moment.

Why don't we button down all the time? Like, for instance, when we don't have to?

Many of us can live more frugally when our situation requires it. And most of us, if we continued to live frugally, would be in a better financial position all around. So why don't we live frugally as our norm?

I don't have the answers. I'm sometimes just as guilty of these things myself.

But the question remains: can we make peace with living like we need to in the lean times, so we can choose to live that way in times of plenty?

Be Honest About the Phase of Life You Are In

We all have hobbies. When a friend told me about a local gun range and their pistol leagues, I excitedly looked into participating. But the registration fee, along with the weekly range fee, was more than I could realistically afford at the time.

Because, life. Because there are three pigs in my barn and a coop full of meat birds that need to be fed.

Because my sons grew again and need shoes (and size 15s aren't cheap). Because we need a brake job on the truck. Because butcher time is coming and we need to fix the chicken plucker.

Because braces. Retainers. Night Guards. Because soon-to-be-teen drivers and auto insurance. Because it's almost time to start CLEPing out of college courses.

I could make a list as long as this chapter, and it all costs money.

And after all that goes through my mind, I think that maybe dumping my money at a gun range isn't supposed to be in the cards right now.

In all honesty, most people who are hardcore into shooting for pleasure in pistol leagues aren't people who worry about how to feed a barn full of animals or pay for teenage boy car insurance.

There is a demographic of people who participate in certain things at certain points in their life. There are times in your life where you won't be able to afford something because of other things that come along with where you are in life. It's okay. Have your moment of frustration but then make a choice. You can either make peace with being in this place or continue to be frustrated about something you can't change—at least, not very quickly.

Maybe you've heard adult children joke that when they lived at home, their parents never had air conditioning, never went out to eat or to the movies...but now that the kids are grown up and gone, the parents are "livin' the life" with central air and eating out almost nightly. And the adult children all ask, *why did you never have that stuff when us kids were at home?*

Because, duh. You and all your siblings were at home. And your parents were paying for football fees and car insurance and another pair of pants when you grew two inches overnight.

This is what explains the empty nester mom who suddenly starts planting a big perennial garden in the front yard or the dad who discovers he really likes golf. It's not necessarily that they've suddenly discovered that perennial gardens and golf exist. It's that now they have the money to pursue those interests.

We all go through it, regardless of the dollar amount of our annual income. Your parents did, you will, and your kids will, too. There are many phases in life that are inherently more expensive and others that are much cheaper.

I mean, has it ever occurred to you why we rarely—if ever—see a famous financial guru with five teens at home? I don't know how it works for other people, but in the circles I run in, when John needs new pants because he's in another growth spurt and Maggie needs different shoes for track and Gabe needs money for the camp he's supposed to attend and Zach needs a new uniform and there's something wrong with Amanda's trumpet, you don't have money to fix the brakes in the second vehicle. Go ahead and buy what you can for those kids at the thrift shop, but that still doesn't mean you're going to have money left to fix the washing machine.

And then—it never fails— an expert will suggest, "You should have put some money in savings for an emergency."

Come on, folks. The most realistic response to that statement from many of us could be, "I did. My entire life is emergency."

The Extras Cost Extra

The more stuff we have in our life, the more money we might see going out.

It would really benefit our pocketbooks (not to mention our sanity) to get rid of the extra stuff in life—and I don't just mean stuff we can put our hands on. I'm also talking about junk in our calendars.

Um, Amy…what?

Stick with me for a second, because I might go a little bit left field here.

You might not think this is related, but I'm gonna toss this out into the open. If your kids are in everything and you are volunteering for everything, it might be affecting your ability to live frugally.

There are financial costs that come along with being busier and doing all the things. When you're busier, you take advantage of conveniences (which are always more expensive). Think about it—there are always little costs that come up when you're out and about.

It's all connected. Frugal living is one big piece of a giant happy life puzzle that really doesn't fit into the puzzle unless it's held in by other pieces—like attitude, responsibility, a decent mindset. When you live frugally and you realize you don't need to have that thing or do that thing, it carries over into other parts of your life.

A reader once told me that she feels she's more frugal when she makes stuff from scratch because it puts her in a mindset of doing things more slowly and asking if she really needs to do or have that thing.

Wouldn't it be cool if there was a thrift store you could donate your extra brain stress and calendar clutter to? We take clothes and shoes and CDs and lamps and casserole dishes that we don't need any more or don't have room for. What would life be like if we could drop off the things we cut out of our calendars as well?

The crazy thing is that while other people might be able to use our shoes and clothes and the books we are done reading, no one is going to walk into a thrift store and say, "Yes! I'd love to take this Big Block of Calendar Time that will take up every Sunday for the next six months!"

You're laughing. Why are you laughing? Because the point is we fill our lives with these kinds of things too, and I can't think of a lot of people that would want to pick them up when we decide we don't need them anymore.

Our lives are so full and yet they don't fill us up. We're buying all the things and we're not even satisfied.

See? It's not about the money. Our money issues almost always start with something that has nothing to do with money.

Saving Money is Not a Contest

Listen, we've all met them. The sanctimonious creeps who turn everything into a contest. If you mention you found a great deal on carrot seeds or winter boots or internet, they will one-up you by saying they found it cheaper or have "learned to live without it".

Gag. I mean, seriously. Gag.

Frugal living is not a contest. We're all on our own journey. For some folks, not buying fast food is a big step. For others, it's going a month without eating meat.

Some people view frugal living as a contest because they have saved more. Others view it as a contest in who has less or whose life is harder. There always has to be a competition, right?

Stop turning frugal living into a contest with others.

The only person you should be competing with in the mighty Battle of Who Saves More is the person you used to be. Are you spending less than you did last month? Score. Here's the thing: you can't compare how much money you're spending with another family. There will always be circumstances or issues that make your situations different. So, stop worrying that your neighbor only spent $150 on groceries last month when you just spent that last week. Worry about you.

Understand that your attitude about frugal living matters.

Instead of being nit-picky, be supportive of others who aren't as far on the journey of frugality as you. There are ways to make suggestions about saving money that are helpful, and there are other ways to make those same suggestions and sound like a jerk. It is important that we all know the difference.

Years ago, I sat in a group of women and the conversation got around to saving money. Everyone was talking about all the things they'd been doing to be more thrifty; some of the women quite obnoxious in their exposition—turning it into a contest, one gal trying to outdo the next. After a bit, a mom in the group mentioned that she'd taken her daughter out for her birthday for ice cream.

Gasp!

You guys, you would have thought the mom said she'd went on a shoe shopping spree or gambled her entire paycheck away at the casino. A good chunk of the women sitting around "politely" blasted the mom for the birthday outing saying *she could have done something cheaper.* As the "polite" comments kept coming, you could see the mom shrink in her chair and totally clam up.

Finally, one gal—who up until that point had remained quiet—said, "You know, ladies? We all take our own path to frugality. Every step matters. We all get there in our own time."

When you're seeking a more simple, frugal life, it is a journey. It takes time. You don't wake up one morning and have all the answers. You can always learn more. And Lord knows, things always come up that put a detour right in the middle of your path. How much more difficult is it to do something like trimming all the fat from your budget when everyone you talk to says you're doing it wrong?

However...

Learn to take advice.

Consider this: someone posts an article online titled *How I Fed My Family on $45 a Week.* How long does it take before someone reads it and immediately starts punching holes in the author's advice?

Usually, not very long at all.

Instead of reading the article and looking for pieces of advice they can put to use in their own life, some readers go into that-would-never-work-for-me-because mode: I have more kids. The cost of living is higher where I am. I can't eat the foods she's suggesting. I don't have the time to do what she's suggesting. It's Tuesday, and the sky is cloudy.

Listen. And believe me when I tell you that I mean this with all the love a homeschooling farmgirl can stick into one sentence: not every article about frugal living is for your life or about your life.

Frugality is personal. When saving money or trying to cut back, we all need to make our own decisions about where to start—and that decision is usually based on lots of other things that people outside our four walls don't get to see. So, take the tips that will help you now. Apply what works, scrap the rest, and move on with your journey of frugal living.

Make peace with where you are. That doesn't mean ignore it. That doesn't mean succumb to it. That doesn't mean give up. That means makes peace with it.

I'm learning the same thing. Where am I? In the middle of that thing where your husband comes home, smiles weakly and asks, "Have you finished that book yet? I hope its soon and that it becomes a best seller." And I know that he's asking because it's easier to dream about that than announce that something is wrong with his truck again that we don't have money to pay for. The kids need their State Shoot entry fee paid and there are turkeys and pheasants to feed and the water pump is making a weird noise.

This is where we are right now. This is our current place in life. And I know that after the heavy sighs and some swallowed profanity, we will readjust and make changes and be flexible.

But I'm not going to lie. Flexibility can make a person sore.

I complained about this to a group of friends, and got this gorgeous piece of advice back from my friend, Donna.

"In the end," she said, "it's the flexibility and the collaboration that proves love is alive. We get through because we either don't have another viable option, or because we choose to do it with grace."

Make peace with yourself and where you are, friends. There are a lot of other people out there in the same boat. And, if it tips over, I'd like to think there is power in numbers when we swim together.

- 8 -

Moving to the Country: The Flip Side of the Frugal Dream

In 2011, my family and I moved to a 5-acre piece of property with a little white house and a big red barn on a dead-end dirt road in Minnesota. I had all the plans to make all the things happen. The gardens would be ginormous. The barn would be filled with animals. I would add grapevines and apple trees and we would convert the unused hay shed into an aquaponics area. We would go off grid.

You guys, we had all the plans.

And over the last several years on our farm, we've done some of these things. Some of these things are still on the to-do list. But the main point of what I'm here to tell you is this: moving to the country is amazing and awesome and completely worth it but it isn't necessarily going to save you money.

Many people are wanting to get away from the city on to a patch of land so they can grow their own and raise their own and be their own. Which is great. But there is a really huge piece of information that a lot of people fail to talk about.

"Our goal is sustainable living on our land, but it still takes more money than we have." — Corey H.

"I believe living frugally while running a farm is a completely different story." — Natalie M.

Living in the country and doing the homesteading thing does not come without expense. I don't want to paint this as a doom and gloom scenario, because that's not what it is at all. I adore living in the country and all the opportunities that we've experienced because of it. But has it been a money saving adventure for us?

Not exactly.

There are some things we need to be honest about, folks.

Growing your own and raising your own means that some of your food costs haven't disappeared, they've just shifted.

My favorite thing to hear people say is that they live more cheaply because they raise their own food. And when you ask them what they spend on food every month, they only give you the cost of what they spend at the grocery store and fail to include the cost of all the things that go into raising their own animals or growing their own food.

To be honest, I love that we can raise our own food out here. I know that many people don't get the opportunity to have apple trees and grapevines and several gardens and a barn full of chickens and pheasants and turkeys and pigs. I wouldn't trade this life for anything and I do feel there is a simplicity and satisfaction here that's hard to put into words.

But let's be clear: there have been months where our bill at the local farm supply store is more than our grocery bill. And that large bill at the local farm supply store would not exist if I wasn't trying to raise my own meat and grow my own veggies and fruit. And while some people might argue that the cost is made up somewhere, I can honestly tell you that no, it isn't always.

Let's look at a couple very simplified, hypothetical examples.

Pretend it's the end of January, and I'm going over our budget. For the month of January, our grocery bill column totals $500. Our farm/garden bill is $100. My garden is buried under snow and the only animals I'm feeding are the breeding stock and layers we over-winter.

Now, let's say it's the end of August. My August grocery bill column is only $200 (because I'm eating from my garden and we butchered a batch of meat birds) but my farm/garden bill is $400. I'm still feeding our breeding stock and layers, but now I have more meat birds and pigs and baby pheasants and some turkeys. And we had to replace some things in our garden...

...And, and, and. Y'all, do you see what I'm getting at?

I can go on social media and tell people that I only spent $200 to feed my family in August and all of social media can be impressed. But in reality, that money was just shifted to be spent on barn/garden stuff. In this very simplified scenario, it's still a total of $600.

Of course, you should realize that most months the total dollar amounts don't balance nicely like that. It's much more heavily weighted one way or the other.

I've had people tell me, "I only spend x amount of dollars on groceries every month. It's so nice to have a freezer already full of meat." And when I ask what that freezer full of meat cost them, they can't answer. I've had people who were so excited that they canned their first batch of strawberry jam, but have no idea how much money went into it. Either they don't know because they haven't figured it out, or it simply didn't occur to them that even though it feels great to go the homemade route, there is still a cost to get that finished product. It's almost as if the costs for raising your own or growing your own are in some financial column that we mean to write down, but never actually do—so they never get accounted for.

Unless you are to the point that you are saving all your seeds to replant for years to come, you're spending money on your garden.

Unless you are to the point where you have a closed system and don't need to buy chicks, kids, calves, or piglets, you're spending money on animals. And unless you're somehow 100% free-ranging/grass feeding you're spending money to feed them. And you may have it whittled down to a minimal amount, but there is a cost. So, let's stop pretending there isn't.

I've had people tell me that the amount they spend on raising chickens or growing watermelons or canning pickles is so minimal, they just don't really keep track. And I get that. But minimal isn't free. "Minimal" things (especially on a homestead or farm) can add up to an amount that has you scratching your head, wondering where your money went.

What Does It Really Mean to Save Money?

I bake a lot of homemade bread. I had someone ask me once, "I love your bread but be honest…does it really save you money to bake your own?"

Well, not if I can get a loaf at the store for 89 cents—especially if you factor in the time it takes me to make it.

Is my bread more awesome? Yeah. Is it cheaper than what I can buy at the store? Not necessarily.

Y'all, I can't put a full homegrown meal on the table for cheaper than generic macaroni and cheese, and neither can you. Sorry.

In the homestead community, people will often joke about the $500 tomato or the $1000 egg. It costs money to produce this stuff at home, and for 99% of us, the costs don't go away. Over time they may decrease—you only have to build a coop once, hopefully—but the cost of feeding animals or growing a garden doesn't completely disappear.

My cousin, Diana, says that while she loves to grow her own tomatoes, there is nothing "cheaper" about doing so. The hot Texas sun beats down on her urban vegetable garden and she uses a lot of water to keep her garden from scorching. *A lot.*

"With the increase in my water bill the first summer I grew tomatoes…let's just say that those were some expensive tomatoes," she said. "And yeah, they taste better right off the vine, but come on. If I can walk to the grocery store and buy a vine with 8 tomatoes on it for $3.99? It's not always cheaper to grow your own."

There are definite qualifications to the whole "homegrown is cheaper" argument.

"We had friends who went from eating as cheaply and unhealthfully as possible in the city to buying a little hobby farm and going completely organic," says Will, who recently moved to his own 10-acre homestead. "They were a little caught off guard by how much their food bill actually increased…even though they were growing and raising much of their food themselves. They were under the impression that if they were growing it themselves, their food bill would go down. They neglected to take into consideration that they were growing *better* food than what they *had* been eating. It would be like taking a leap from eating Ramen to eating organic kale and grass-fed beef. There is an obvious cost increase there, even if you're raising it yourself."

If you factor in electricity, vet bills, repairs to buildings or fences you wouldn't even have if you weren't raising or growing your own food—not to mention all the other surprises that come up—your adventure as a homesteader might not be saving you as much as you assumed it would.

If you're looking for honesty: in the time we've been here at the farm, I can tell you some years we've just about broke even. Other years we've definitely been in the red. Part of that is where we are in our journey. Another part of it is just the unpredictability of life on a farm.

And yes, the food tastes better and might be better for you. But to the folks who think moving to a homestead will always be a money-saving adventure…there's way more to the story than you got in the last romanticized internet post you read.

"Coming from the city, I think we had a romanticized vision of what life in the country would be like," says country living newbie, Alexis. "There is just this huge…almost like, religious movement to get out and away from city life where you can have all this freedom. You're going to have all these chickens and a couple goats and a huge garden and then all of a sudden you don't know where all your money went. I mean, it's worth it…but it's definitely not as cheap as some people make it seem."

Or as her husband put it, "The *idea* of moving to the country is way less expensive than actually *doing it*."

I realize there are many factors to this. A lot of how much you save by moving to the country and trying your hand at homesteading will have to do with how you eat, where you live, your specific property, the specific issues or non-issues of a certain year, the growing season and what weather you got, how you're used to shopping…all sorts of things. It's also a bit of trial and error. We've learned a lot about better ways to do things financially and organizationally since we moved here. My point is there's way more involved in the "raise your own food and you're going to save money!" than what many people will spout off.

A Big Piece of Property Requires Money to Take Care of It

I remember looking at much larger pieces of property when we were ready to purchase our farm—until it occurred to us that more property meant more money to take care of it. Bigger pieces of land require bigger machinery to work it. Bigger operations with more animals require more feed to keep things running.

"The thing that floored me," says Brent, who recently moved to the country, "was how much gas it takes to mow lawn. We went from a little postage stamp yard in the city to 3 acres of yard in the country...holy moly. I felt like we were running to get more gas every single week just to keep the lawn under control."

If you're in charge of a piece of property that requires the use of ATVs, tractors, skid loaders, or other large machinery, those all take fuel to run. And when they need maintenance or repair? Dollar signs, y'all. Even if you have the know-how to fix it, you still need parts to get the job done.

The property itself can be more expensive just because of the logistics of nature within that space. If a storm goes through, you've got way more land damage to deal with. If you're dealing with drought or flooding, you've got a larger piece of work in front of you.

"Land maintenance is expensive and it's usually not something you can just avoid to save money. Mowing large lawns, cutting up fallen or dead trees, fencing, and clearing all cost money and/or time," Meredith explains.

"People just don't realize how expensive it is to get a farm set up - fence, barn, sheds, coops, etc." says Bonnie.

Brandy adds, "There are equipment repairs, machinery purchases, fencing maintenance/construction, well repairs…"

The list goes on, y'all.

A Property with Outbuildings is Like Having More Than One House

I remember the first time we got our electric bill on the farm. I was absolutely floored. It was over $300 more than what we had paid at our place in town.

But that will happen when you're providing electric to other buildings or using heat lamps or have multiple pumps on the property to run water to different buildings.

"Moving to the country means that you're not just providing utilities and upkeep to a house and a garage," Teresa points out. "The barn(s) and other outbuildings take a piece of the pie, too."

DIY Isn't Always Cheaper

The funny thing is that people often think of homesteaders and farmers as the ultimate do-it-yourselfers. The folks who can fix anything with a piece of duct tape and some baling twine. Folks, the reason they got so handy at punting and fixing things like that was out of necessity. It wasn't because they were on some no-buy challenge and had to come up with a different way to fix things. It's because the money they had went to fix something else that came up and now there's no money to fix this thing.

"Homestead things are expensive sometimes, particularly if you're not mechanically apt or if you are pressed for time," Thomas explains. "There are a lot of DIY or fix-it projects that will save money, but finding the time and the 'cheap' materials to do it is just not always feasible."

And what if you can't fix it yourself?

"We knew lots of maintenance things would be more expensive when we bought the farm," Megan admits, "but no one warned us about how plumbers, HVAC, and septic were so much harder to find. Literally, there are zero plumbing companies located in an hour's drive. We pay $150-200 more for any repair service just because of drive time."

Time is Money

Does raising your own animals for meat save money?

I don't know. What is your time worth?

We butcher all of our own meat here at the homestead. To me, it's not worth the hassle of transporting live animals and the cost to have someone else butcher and process them when we can take a day or two to take care of the task ourselves. It definitely saves us money.

But, yo. It takes time.

Many people don't count the time it takes to do something into their homesteading costs, but y'all, time is real. In fact, available time is one of the reasons you either can or can't do what you want to as a homesteader. If I was working full-time outside the home, I wouldn't be doing nearly as much baking or cooking from scratch, my gardens would be about 1/8 the size of what they currently are, and our barns would have way less animals—if we had any at all.

Barn chores—morning and night—take time. Planting and weeding and harvesting takes time. General upkeep around the homestead takes time. Processing and putting up food takes time. Animal emergencies take time. Pretending that all people should have the time to do all the things that need to be done on a successful homestead means you've lost sight of the value (and blessing) of the time you're available to spend doing these things.

Making Money in the Country

But, Amy! You can make money in the country! I'm going to move to the country and sell all my goods!

That's wonderful. I really hope that you do!

But.

The success of selling the wonderful things that you grow and raise will completely depend on how far out in the country you live and who/what is around you. As a very blanket statement (and this may depend on what area of the country you live), most of the people that are going to pay top dollar for your goods are located in more urban areas. If you want to sell to them, you have to drive to where they are.

Which, of course, means leaving all your work on the homestead.

Also, keep in mind that if you moved to the country to try your hand at homesteading, you might end up with a lot of other people who moved to the country to try their hand at homesteading. Which means you're all doing the same thing. You can't sell eggs to your neighbor if your neighbor is trying to sell eggs to you. It's not as easy to sell homegrown pork if there are four other hog farmers in a 15-mile radius.

I chatted once with a local about this topic. She sells her farm raised produce (veggies and meat) to a couple of the higher end restaurants within a 50-mile radius of her home. She said she wasn't sure why people didn't put more effort into selling their goods the way she was. I saw her point, but also had to point out that there are more far more free-range chicken farmers in the area than there are restaurants serving that product.

Also, I will say this from personal experience: On one end of the homesteading spectrum is the ability to provide for yourself. The other end of the spectrum is where you're effectively and reliably providing enough to sell to other people. The gray area between the two ends of the spectrum is *huge*. To make a long story short, your farm has to be a certain size before you're going to do anything more than break even with the product you're putting out.

A bit of honesty? Most of us aren't moving to the country to have farms that big.

Some Frugal Tips Don't Work for Folks in the Country

There are many money saving tips that work much better for one group of people than another. "Grow your own food! Plant a garden! Raise some chickens!" are often cited as money-saving hints. But they're not a reality for some folks—at least not on the scale they'd like them to be. Oftentimes, I'll hear from people in apartments who say, "I don't have the space to grow very much food" or folks in an urban area who say, "Yeah, must be nice to actually be allowed to have a pig..."

Yes, there are some things that work in the country that just won't fly in the middle of the city. But to keep things fair, there are just as many money-saving hints that aren't a reality for those who live in the country. For instance:

Give up your daily fancy coffee!

"I always think it is funny when they suggest giving up 'your daily Starbucks coffee'", says Summer, who doesn't live anywhere near a Starbucks.

"Ha!" agrees Sari. "It's so rare that I even see a Starbucks or a Caribou that I have always considered getting a fancy coffee as a treat. Are there really people who stop every single day?"

Walk everywhere!

Truth is, it's 10 miles (30 miles, 45 miles) to the nearest grocery store. Now, I am smart and try to plan my runs to town accordingly. For instance, I head to the grocery store on Wednesday or Sunday because that's when I'm already in town for church. But this whole walking everywhere you need to go? No, y'all. It just doesn't work out here.

Get a smaller car!

Depends. This makes great sense if you're spending a lot of time commuting back and forth to work and don't need the space to cart kids around. But I can't haul hay, wood shavings, or bulk feed in the back of a little Ford Fiesta. And I'm pretty sure those babies don't come with a tow package...

Shop around! Clip coupons!

A lot of folks who have made the decision to move to the country have some sort of moral/ethical/health food type mojo going on. I can't remember the last time I clipped a coupon (other than ones that come specifically from the grocer we shop at, and even then, there aren't a lot that we use.) When I go to the grocery store, I'm looking for flour and sugar. I'm looking for vegetables and fruit. I'm looking for a lot of stuff in bulk or things that don't have bar codes. Tell me: when was the last time you saw a coupon for stuff like that?

The other thing about couponing is that to take advantage of some of the cost savings, you have to drive from store to store to get the best deal.

"That whole 'shop around for the lowest prices' thing?" Grace says, with a sigh. "(We have) one store 30 minutes away. *One*."

Besides there being a drive to the store, another rural or small-town problem is that when you don't have a big choice for local stores, the prices at the local store often reflect that.

"Grocery prices are pretty inflated in my small-town grocery store," says Mandy. "I've really had to learn prices of grocery items to know what's a good deal or not. I usually have to save my big grocery trips for when I drive to the nearest 'big' city and only shop essentials and sales at my hometown store."

Darcy shares, "When we moved from Chicago to rural Central Illinois 2 years ago, I was shocked by how much food costs out here. I could drive to Chicago, stock up, and drive back and—even with gas costs—pay less."

Compare prices on internet providers!

I remember the struggle my good friend had when her daughter was doing online college in high school. She had to choose classes based on how much data the videos or online labs would take from their cell phone plan, or her daughter would have to drive to the library and schedule time on their computers. When my friend mentioned this, the advisor was floored. The advisor had never heard of someone living in an area where they didn't have wi-fi right at their house.

It happens. It's a reality. Living out in the country, you might only have one provider to choose from. In fact, some folks are so far out (or happen to be in a randomly located hole) that there is no wi-fi and you're stuck with a data sucking hot spot or iffy dish.

Looking at online school? Running a business from home? Working on that great blog or publishing a bunch of e-books? Internet might be more spendy and/or less awesome than you'd hoped.

Cut Cable! Stream your TV shows!

Wait, people still pay for cable? I thought everyone was streaming from Netflix now.

Not in the country.

"We are on satellite internet, so our bandwidth is limited and we can do little to no streaming. And we can't even get local tv channels without satellite tv," says Bonnie.

Cut your landline!

Some of you are giggling right now because you didn't think there were homes that still have landlines. I mean, didn't landlines stop being a thing in the early 2000s?

Again, not in the country.

"We can't cut our landline because we get very poor cell phone service," Bonnie explains.

"We are required to have a landline at our place in the country because it's the only way we can get internet where we live. Yes, for real. In 2017," Kurt says.

Life in the country, y'all. It's a different kind of thing.

Listen. We all have stuff to pay for regardless of where we live. We all have things that come up and expensive issues we need to deal with regardless of where we call home. There are many people doing the self-sufficient homesteader thing who are struggling with money just as much as someone living in the heart of the nearest metropolis.

There are lots of people out there who are wondering how to get by. Some of those people are filling their freezer with pork and chicken they raised on their homestead, and some of those people brown bag their lunch for a job they walk to in a suit and tie.

We're more alike than we like to think, folks.

For some people, moving to the country and doing the homesteading thing is more about a mind-set. A fellow homesteader and I got around to talking one day about the choice to homestead and whether or not it actually saves money.

"I laugh every time someone tells me they're gonna buy a little piece of property and be a homesteader because they're gonna save money," Maggie said. "I mean, there is so much stuff that comes up out here that has to be paid for, and you can't really comprehend it until it's in front of you."

"So, you would say that moving to the country *doesn't* save money?" I asked.

"I would say that life costs money no matter *where* you live," she said. "When you add everything up, I don't know that raising my own meat birds actually saves me a whole ton of money. But my chickens taste better than what I can get at the store, and I know being out here has saved my sanity. And honestly? *That's* worth every penny."

- 9 -

Saving Money Takes Time

One of the most interesting things to witness as a parent is how your kids deal with money. When your kids get to a certain age, suddenly they want bigger things. And while this is great because it generally means they've moved past cheap plastic junk and moved into more lasting things with a purpose, it generally also means that these things cost a lot more money.

My sons both like computers and decided at some point that they both needed to build their own desktops. This required hours of research and planning regarding each piece and part that would go into building the computers they'd always wanted. There were many lessons learned, like cost comparison, the importance of shopping around, and how it's sometimes just as good to buy something that isn't name brand.

But the biggest lesson came when one of my sons was down to the last piece he needed to build the desktop of his dreams: the processor. He'd saved money for the rest of the parts and was now waiting on this one. It was spendy. And this, friends, is where another lesson came in.

"Mom? I need $250."

"That's great," I said. "Save your allowance."

"But it will literally take like half a year to save that much money."

"Well, you've got to figure out a way to make more money quicker then."

My son then told me that he would be happy to work doing extra jobs (above and beyond his weekly responsibilities) for extra pay. I told him that was great, but I had no extra money to give him.

He stared at me blankly.

"But I'd be willing to do more work."

"Yep. I get it. But there is only so much money in the well, son. You're gonna have to branch out and make money elsewhere."

He asked around to neighbors, family, and friends. Job offers came in, but most of them were the future *he can mow for me every week* or *he can help me with the next load of hay*. Great opportunities for him, but he'd have to wait at least three months from the frozen snowy world we were sitting in.

And so...he waited.

Making money takes time. Saving money takes time. Making a change in our budget takes time.

Now, you may kindly smile and think of this as a kid's story. And it sorta is. But maybe that's only because the kid doesn't have access to a credit card or the ability to put himself in debt for the thing he wants right now. Maybe it's only a kid story because due to his age (and his parents' inability to front him the money) he actually has to save cash for what he wants.

It's maybe also a kid's story because in the middle of my son saving money for the computer processor, he didn't have to worry about additional life costs like buying food or gas or surprise costs like parts to fix the washing machine or the broken pipe in the barn.

Saving Money Takes Time Because Life is Still Happening

We are always working hard to save money for upcoming projects on the farm. I was actually thinking about our to-do list as I loaded bags of feed into the back of my truck. I thanked the employee who was helping me and told him to have a nice day.

I got back in the truck, and it wouldn't start.

One hour and a phone call to my hubby later, we determined the starter on the truck had suddenly died.

I mean, who knew the starter can just…die? Not me.

Replacing the starter in our truck was obviously not in our plans, and even though my husband did all the work himself, it still set us back a chunk of cash for the part.

That cash was pulled from other places. While we can be thankful the cash was available to be pulled from something else, the fact is, *the cash got pulled from something else*—something else we'd now be behind on accomplishing.

This is how most of us live—at least the people in my social circle. Forget xM radio and daily pumpkin spice lattes. My peeps are trying to figure out how to pay for an emergency tooth extraction in the midst of trying to replace the full-of-food freezer that died.

Is that where you live, too?

Can I get an amen?

Amen.

Financial gurus talk a lot about saving. Sometimes that is attained by not spending as much, and sometimes it is accomplished by taking a little bit from each paycheck and setting it aside. And that's all really great advice.

But it's frustrating—and I'm probably preaching to the choir—to think about setting aside $20 from this week's paycheck when the underwire in your one bra just poked through—again—and you're actually going to have to purchase a new one—for $20.

It's hard to get excited about financial advice from someone who just keeps saying you should *pay yourself first* and *put x amount of dollars back every week.* I mean, I get it if you can maybe choose to not buy another hanging basket of petunias to decorate your front porch. But what if your reality means you can't set anything aside this week—again—because you're paying for the repair of a leaking toilet and dear God, is that *another* fee from the school?

Trust me, I understand the purpose behind an emergency fund, and we love to have that money sitting. It's just that when we do have that money sitting, it's almost as if the appliances, vehicles, and members of the barn get together for a pow-wow and shake dice to see who will be the next jerk face with their grubby little fat fingers in the mason jar of cash we've hidden.

I mean, that can't just be how it works at *our* house.

It's great to have money saved up and sitting. It's a beautiful thing when it happens. It's great that when something comes up, you have money sitting to pay for it.

But in real life, when the money *is* sitting, it isn't always spent on the thing it was intended for. This is a hard thing to come to terms with, because when our purpose is to save money to go towards something specific (like replacing the roof on the chicken coop or buying a new math curriculum), we don't want to spend that saved money on an emergency furnace repair or new tires.

I know. I totally know this. It's like the money you scrimped to save or worked extra hours to come up with becomes sparkly and earmarked for The Thing You Want to Spend It On. And you almost feel as both you and The Thing You Want to Spend It On have been violated when that money has to be given to a plumber who makes an emergency visit at 7 am.

But here's the thing.

Even though the money you saved was supposed to be reserved for The Thing You Want to Spend It On, it's still (in a roundabout way) going to help you get to that item. If you have the money sitting and can pay cash for the emergency repair, it means you're not using a credit card and incurring debt. And less debt means you're closer to The Thing You Want.

I know. That doesn't really make it any less sucktastic when you're standing there with the $300 you've saved to build a fodder system and now you're handing it over to the mechanic. There is still pain and frustration and maybe even disgust when you let those dollar bills fall into someone else's hand.

You're totally allowed to have some time to be mad about that.

But trust me. Sophie the Chicken wants you to be strong. And she's rootin' for you.

Saving Money is Not a Simple Mathematical Formula

Algebra can be tough to learn, but at least there is a formula. The sides are balanced. There is a right and wrong answer. Input this, output that. The equation, when solved, makes sense.

Our problem is we assume that saving money is a mathematical formula. If we save x dollars (y weeks), it should equal a certain amount of money at a certain point in time.

But anyone who has tried this knows it doesn't always work that easily. In fact, saving money is more like a video game. It's like we're on a path, collecting all the coins but then there is a glitch and the game starts over and we are back to square one.

I mean, what the actual what?

Where Is the Extra Money?

Financial gurus keep talking about saving our extra money.

What is this extra money they speak of? I'm confused, because at our house there is always somewhere for all of our funds to go.

Saving money takes time because any change takes time. Life is still throwing punches in the midst of the positive modifications you're trying to make. And the crazy thing is that even though some things will clearly get better, you may not see a big difference in your bottom line.

I remember standing at the laundry line hanging a load of clothes one morning and imagining how nice it would be to always buy from local farmers when purchasing produce we wanted but didn't grow in our own garden, and meat that we didn't raise on our farm.

Why don't we do that now? We do when we can, but it's not something we can always do. Nine and a half times out of ten, the local stuff is more expensive, and there is only ever so much money in my pocket.

When I look at my bank account and envision how much more money we'd need to save or earn per month in order to primarily shop local and/or organic, one point stands out to me: if we were ever to get to that point, we still wouldn't have any *extra* money left over at the end of the month.

Does that make sense? Do you understand what I'm saying there?

Let's say that being able to afford eating the way I'd like to eat means that I have to either make or save $300 a month in order to reliably afford that. And let's say that I finally afford that by making or saving more money, and find myself able to supplement what we can't grow or raise ourselves by buying all locally grown veggies and meat and honey.

Go me! Yes! Homesteader goal attained!

But guess what?

I still have no *extra* money. I've found the $300 somehow to cover the cost of the food...but there is *still no extra money at the end of the week.*

Now yes, we would be eating better. And yes, we would be supporting the local economy. And both of those points are valid and worthy. But the fact remains we wouldn't necessarily be changing our *financial* situation. We wouldn't have any *more* money left over at the end of the month.

For people who are frugal for simple living/health/moral reasons, that maybe doesn't matter—you feel you've bettered your life and the end justifies the means. But if your goal in frugal living was to have more money to put in savings each month, you actually haven't changed a thing at all.

There is always something to spend money on, right? Some of us are living with such a back log of items we want to accomplish or things we want to add to our lives for whatever reason that when we have an extra $20 or $200 or $2000 we go accomplish those things or add those things to our lives. Which is great.

But guess what? We're not necessarily any further ahead financially. And we still probably don't have any extra money left at the end of the month.

"But you're buying better food! But you're driving a more reliable car! But you can afford violin lessons!"

Yes. And I still don't have any more money leftover at the end of the week. Or the place that we just got to (yay!) has added expenses that we didn't count on and the breathing space we thought we'd made in our budget has been taken up by new stuff (no!).

So, what would you do with an extra $20?

When some people think about having extra money, they think about putting it towards a vacation fund or a remodel or even donating it to a certain charity. These are all great things.

With extra money, other people will stock their pantry with groceries or put more meat in their freezer. These are also great ideas.

But, to still other folks, having extra money in their pocket means they're telling their kid *yes, they actually can go on the overnight speech trip.* Or they get to replace a drawer full of underwear or socks that are particularly drafty.

Extra means something different to different people. Or maybe *extra* is determined by where you are in life. I read extra as "not earmarked for anything else" or "no specific place this has to go." And some of us are at a point in life where all of our dollar bills are earmarked for so many different things, they're permanently creased and falling apart.

I recently asked my social media followers and friends what they would do if they suddenly had an extra $20. Lots of people answered. Some people privately messaged me.

"My son needs pants. Not a specific brand of pants. I'm talking about something to cover the bottom half of his body so he can be allowed in public places. If he was average height and weight, it wouldn't be an issue. He wears a 30x34. Tall, skinny, and hard to find pants for at a thrift shop."

"You know what I'd like? A new bra. Doesn't that sound stupid? If I had $20 that wasn't going to something for the house or the fridge or the kids, I'd buy a new bra and throw away the stretched out worthless one I'm currently wearing."

The main problem is this: it's like we're being told to take that extra money we'd normally blow on something frivolous and do something responsible with it, like put it in savings.

Yes, if you're blowing your money, be an adult and put some of it back into savings. But seriously, last time I checked, buying underwear for a growing kid so they don't have elastic imprints on their waist anymore is not blowing your money.

What's also interesting is what people categorize as an *unexpected expense*, which I think also says something about where you are financially or how you view money. When I asked folks on social media to share "the last unexpected expense" they had to deal with, many people talked about large expenses—some that happened a year or more earlier.

An acquaintance messaged me and said, "I think these people have a different idea of 'unexpected'. Maybe I'm on more of a fixed income than them. My answer was going to be 'the last unexpected expense I had to deal with was a tank of gas to be with my mom after her emergency surgery', but after reading everyone else's answers, I'll just keep that one between you and me."

Things might get worse before they get better.

Sometimes when we talk about frugality or saving money, we unknowingly frame it with this assumption in the back of our mind: *I will reach a point when I won't have to think about or struggle with money anymore.*

There might be a few people in the world that get to live that way. But for the majority of us? No. We're never going to get to the point that money doesn't take up some part of our brain.

Saving money takes time. Learning to live frugally takes time. Feeling like you're making any headway takes time. Life happens. Stuff gets added. Things change. It's a constant search for balance.

The crazy thing about saving money is that sometimes when you're doing what you should, it may appear that your "quality of life" is going down. In other words, even though you're actually improving your life, it may appear to yourself and others that your quality of life is decreasing.

If the only way you can afford to go out to eat or see the concert or get into the museum or purchase beer for the party is by using credit cards, and you decide that as part of your new frugal lifestyle you're not going to run your credit cards—let's be honest. Your life is going to look a lot different while you're making adjustments.

When the sump pump stops running or you have to cover a surprise ER bill with the cash you had saved, the funds suddenly aren't there for the new uniforms you need for work. Without credit cards, you're gonna have to be uber creative to figure out how to remedy those situations.

Saving money takes time and it may appear (or feel like) your quality of life stays down for quite a while. Until, of course, the change becomes your new normal.

That's not to say that living frugally sucks or that you should become a beat down, hollow shell of a person who dramatically sighs about the things you can't have. It definitely takes a perspective change to see the benefits in living frugally and not be Captain Crabby about the things you can't do.

And all of that? That, my friends, takes time.

Again, Time is Money

One of the most common complaints I hear about money saving suggestions is most practices or tips that are supposed to save you money take too much time. Money saving and time saving are usually not found in the same sentence. Convenience is helpful, but often more expensive.

I remember talking to a friend one time about baking bread. I told her it's not that hard and I enjoy doing it. She said, "If I ever figure out a day that I have a three-hour stretch at home, you can teach me how to make some."

Touché.

Meal planning takes time. Shopping the sales takes time. It all takes time and for a majority of society, they just don't have any to spare.

I spent three hours making noodles one day. True, it wasn't a constant 3 hours, some of that was drying time and while the noodles were drying, I was outside working in the barn. But let's be real. I could have gone to the store and bought the noodles I needed for 88 cents.

I enjoy making noodles, but I'd also like to think my time is worth a lot more than 88 cents.

Sometimes the money-making or money-saving thing isn't worth your time. There is a plasma donation center local to us, but the financial compensation one receives from donating plasma only makes sense if they aren't traveling 90 minutes one way to do it. Driving around to find the sales or use the coupons only makes sense if you're not spending more in gas than what you're saving on the items you're buying.

Time is money—in varying amounts to different people.

Listen. We're all busy, we are just busy in different ways. I don't care if you have one kid, ten kids, babies, teenagers, no kids, you're retired, or you just graduated college. It doesn't matter. We all live full lives. We've all got 24 hours in the day and most of us could use 36 to get everything done.

But, even though we are all busy, our lives are set up differently. Being busy at home is different than being busy at a job with a boss who can fire you if you don't show up. So, while I never lack for things to do while running a farm, homeschooling our kids, and operating a home business, I have options available to me with my set up that someone who works outside the home doesn't have. Me telling you to cook everything from scratch doesn't make a whole lot of sense if you work 60 hours a week away from home.

Know how I know that? It's because if I worked 60 hours a week away from home, I wouldn't be spending my Sunday off cooking from scratch. Or maybe I'd try to, but it would be lumped in with all the other household things I'd need to get done because it was my day at home.

Or, you know, maybe I'd just want to sit and relax.

I'm not here to tell you which money saving tips are best. I don't know your life. What I do know is that we need to:

> a) be realistic about what tips would make sense in our own individual homes and understand that

some of them, although uncomfortable, might actually work.

b) realize that the same specific tips don't work in every home, and it's not just because someone doesn't want to put the effort forth.

If a certain tip works for us in our situation, great. If it doesn't work for someone else, it doesn't necessarily mean they are lazy and totally suck.

Seriously.

(And if you just pulled a *yeah, but* after reading that, please visit chapter two again.)

The point is that saving money does take time…but time is also money. And we have to figure out for ourselves within our own situations how to successfully tightrope walk between those two points.

Saving Money is Like Dieting

Deciding to live a frugal life and wanting to save money is kind of like deciding to start a diet. In both instances, we make the choice to cut back on something, and often in the beginning we can be pretty hardcore about it.

You do really well for a while and then…something happens. In the diet world, it's a cute kid offering you a piece of birthday cake. In frugal world, it's something that breaks or needs to be replaced, like tires or a bathroom fan or a window.

In both cases, we eat the cake or spend the money and think *fine, it doesn't even matter anymore. I failed. I might as well quit.* And you eat two pieces of birthday cake and a whole tub of ice cream—or you go to Target and buy candles and sharpies and chalkboard quote boxes for your walls.

You give up because it's hard. You give up because you feel like it's not worth it. You give up because you look at what's happening and feel like you're not making headway. You give up because you feel like one stumble messes up the whole race.

I know this happens, you guys. I've seen it with my own eyes. Maybe sometimes by looking in the mirror.

Just like with dieting we want results to be noticeable, quantifiable, but most of all immediate. But just like with dieting, there is no quick fix. The biggest thing we need to learn for frugality is patience. If you're reading this book looking for the quick easy fix, the gold ticket money-saving tip, the way to fix it all by tomorrow, it doesn't exist. I'm sorry. And anyone who tells you it *does*—whether they're talking about dieting or frugal living—is scheming to get your hard-earned dollars.

Also, they're *completely full of it.*

Saving money takes time. Saving money requires patience and an understanding that the non-awesome surprises of life are still happening in the midst of the awesome money saving, budget plumping thing you're trying to do.

And sometimes the key to surviving is just someone having the compassion to say that if that's where you are right now, a) you're not imagining it and b) you don't suck.

Thanks.

You're welcome.

About the Author

Amy Dingmann is a quirky homeschooling farmgirl from central Minnesota who enjoys strong coffee, red wine, and ice cream with marshmallows on top. She lives with three really tall guys, two of whom she gave birth to.

Amy is made up of equal parts compassion, sass, and slap-yo'-face truth. She's so glad that you've joined her for a real, authentic, and hilariously truthful look at life with money.

Amy regularly writes at her sites afarmishkindoflife.com and thehmmmschoolingmom.com, and loves to connect with readers on social media through the Facebook pages associated with those sites.

She is also the author of *The Homeschool Highway: How to Navigate Your Way Without Getting Carsick*, available on Amazon.

Questions? Comments? Feel free to email Amy at:

amy@afarmishkindoflife.com

Enjoyed the book? Leave a review at Amazon!